Outdoor Learning through the Seasons

Outdoor play experiences have a crucial role in young children's learning and development and should be a daily part of their lives. Planning and facilitating rich play and learning opportunities outside can, however, be challenging, especially in difficult weather conditions. *Outdoor Learning through the Seasons* provides detailed guidance on how we can encourage young children to engage with the natural world throughout the year.

Using the four seasons as a framework, the book aims to help all adults to feel confident about taking children outside every day and developing their awareness of the world around them. It suggests a wide range of experiences and looks at the various ways in which children can interact with the environment to further their learning and development. There are ideas to brighten grey winter days as well as summer sunshine, snow, wind and rain.

Features include:

- reference to recent research on the significance of outdoor play in early childhood
- guidance on how to encourage effective learning outdoors
- practical tips to offer high quality provision in layout, design and planting
- suggestions for planning outdoor experiences in the seven areas of learning in line with the revised Early Years Foundation Stage
- advice on working with parents and the role of adults
- ideas for all seasons, weather conditions and working with the four elements: earth, air, water and fire
- useful reference lists of further resources including stories, poems and websites
- an appendix of seasonal recipes.

Including a **full-colour photo plate section** to illustrate good practice, this practical book is essential reading for all those looking to provide rich and stimulating outdoor play provision for children in early years settings on a daily basis.

Ann Watts is an early years consultant and leads training for early years managers and practitioners on how to develop their outdoor areas and meet the requirements of the EYFS. She is also a facilitator and trainer with Learning through Landscapes. Her previous publications include *Every Nursery Needs a Garden* (Routledge, 2011).

Outdoor Learning through the Seasons

An essential guide for the early years

Ann Watts

Routledge
Taylor & Francis Group

LONDON AND NEW YORK

First published 2013
by Routledge
2 Park Square, Milton Park, Abingdon, Oxon OX14 4RN

Simultaneously published in the USA and Canada
by Routledge
711 Third Avenue, New York, NY 10017

Routledge is an imprint of the Taylor & Francis Group, an informa business

British Library Cataloguing in Publication Data
A catalogue record for this book is available from the British Library

Library of Congress Cataloging in Publication Data
A catalog record for this book has been requested

ISBN: 978-0-415-65629-0 (hbk)
ISBN: 978-0-415-65630-6 (pbk)
ISBN: 978-0-203-07800-6 (ebk)

Typeset in Optima
by Saxon Graphics Ltd, Derby

MIX
Paper from
responsible sources
FSC® C018575

Printed and bound in Great Britain by MPG Printgroup

Contents

Acknowledgements   vii

Introduction   1

Part One
Outdoor learning and the Early Years Foundation Stage   5

1   **Characteristics of effective learning**   7

2   **Creating an enabling environment outdoors – design, layout and planting**   17

3   **Creating an enabling environment outdoors – areas of learning**   29

4   **Working in partnership with parents**   45

Part Two
The four seasons   57

5   **Spring**   59

6   **Summer**   75

7   **Autumn**   93

8   **Winter**   107

Part Three
The four elements   129

9   **Earth**   131

10   **Air**   139

11 Water   147

12 Fire   161

Conclusion   165

Bibliography   169

Appendix: Recipes for every season   171

Acknowledgements

I would like to express grateful thanks to the staff, parents and children in all the following early years settings for welcoming me in and giving permission to take and use photographs for this book:

Bayonne Nursery School and Rouzanna Children's Centre
Crosfield Nursery School and Children's Centre
KISH Kindergarten
Major Minors Day Nursery
Nutfield Day Nursery
Peter Pan Preschool Nursery
St Michaels' Community Nursery
Treetots Under Fives
Tunstall Nursery School and Children's Centre

Also to my wonderful grandchildren – Joshua, Harry and Lucy – whose deep involvement and enthusiasm for the natural world inspired my work.

Introduction

The importance of outdoor learning for young children was first recognised by the pioneers of nursery education. Froebel devised the word 'kindergarten' meaning 'children's garden', and Margaret McMillan continued to establish what were generally known as 'open-air nursery schools'. She, too, recognised the garden and outdoor space not just as a place where children could run around, but somewhere that offered experiences which contributed to a child's learning and development. She described it as a classroom roofed only by the sky. In her gardens she provided low walls, stepping stones and logs so that 'children could play bravely and adventurously'. Ropes and trees were thought to be the best climbing apparatus you could have (McMillan 1919: 23).

From 1960 to 1980 however there was less focus on being outdoors. When new nurseries were opened during this period, they often had a tarmac or safety surface space with fixed climbing apparatus and an array of bicycles, trucks and scooters. Little thought was given to interaction with the natural environment, the plants and the wildlife. Now, however the importance of outdoor learning has emerged with more urgency, as research evidence demonstrates not just the importance of being outside, but also the need to become physically and emotionally involved with the natural world around us.

This book highlights the incredibly rich learning resource that is offered by the environment itself. It is dynamic and ever-changing. There is a timeless sense of rhythm and order. Sometimes this is interrupted by unnatural weather conditions, and the book suggests ways of being prepared to maximise these additional learning opportunities.

In a study by Faber Taylor *et al.* (2001) it was found that exposure to nature reduced the symptoms of ADHD in children three-fold compared with staying indoors. Later studies have concluded that exposure to the natural environment gives all children a greater sense of self-worth and a reduction in stress and aggressive behaviour levels (Bird 2007). In 2005, Richard Louv gave us the phrase 'Nature Deficit Disorder', which described the 'human costs of alienation from nature, among them, diminished use of the senses, attention difficulties, and higher rates of physical and emotional illnesses' (quoted in Moss 2012: 2).

The National Trust and the RSPB have both commissioned major reports that detail the adverse effects of a childhood without access to a natural environment and the experiences it offers. Stephen Moss writes in *Natural Childhood* that 'Our nation's children are missing out on the pure joy of connection with the natural world' (2012: 2). Part of the problem is that adults no longer allow children to play out as maybe they once did. Children do not roam freely and consequently are missing out on many of the joys and pleasures of childhood. He argues that as a nation we need to 'kick start a new way of life for our children by reconnecting them with nature once again' (2012: 3).

Another recent report, *Sowing the seeds – reconnecting London's children with nature* (Greater London Authority 2011), acknowledges the benefits of play-orientated engagement with nature. It focuses on the goal of 'offering children engaging everyday nature experiences, that give children exploratory, play orientated, hands on contact with nature, not just didactic or curriculum related activities' (2011: 3). A key recommendation is that 'Schools and early years settings should give greater emphasis to offering children engaging everyday nature experiences within their grounds' (2011: 6).

This book aims to redress some of the above issues. It will enable practitioners to offer these everyday experiences within their own grounds wherever possible. It also offers suggestions for settings that have little or no space they can call their own. Venturing further afield into local green spaces on a regular basis can be rewarding for both adults and children. Working with children outdoors every day requires adults to be resourceful and flexible. Children enjoy being outside: it seems natural for them to want to go out at every possible opportunity. It is, therefore, important that adults are able to respond in a similar way. They, too, need to enjoy being outside. This book offers ways to encourage adults and children to become more involved with the natural world throughout the year.

Part One is written for all Foundation Stage practitioners as it is directly concerned with the revised Early Years Foundation Stage (EYFS).

Chapter 1 emphasises the importance of being able to observe how children learn, rather than what they learn. The outdoor space is well suited to giving opportunity for this. Children have more freedom and become engaged in deep-level play and exploration. The characteristics of effective learning are detailed with reference to the outdoor environment and how they are able to maximise opportunities for effective learning

Chapter 2 is concerned with layout, design and planting. There are practical tips to offer high quality provision for sand, water and mud play as well as den-building. It refers to growing spaces for flowers and vegetables. There are ideas for seasonal planting for both small and large spaces, as well as plants that can be used to supply natural play materials.

Chapter 3 refers to the areas of learning in the revised EYFS. It offers suggestions that will ensure you can offer exciting learning experiences and outdoor opportunities for children to develop in the three prime areas and the four specific areas of learning.

In Chapter 4, the importance of working closely with parents is emphasised and there are ideas to encourage parents to take their children outdoors on a regular basis. A case study shows how very young children and their parents benefit from weekly outdoor sessions in the local park.

Parts Two and Three are written for all adults who are involved with young children and are concerned to offer them the very best childhood experiences. Many adults have recollections and memories of a sense of freedom and fun, and are concerned that children today no longer have this freedom. Rachel Carson (1956: back cover) writes:

> If a child is to keep alive his inborn sense of wonder—he needs the companionship of at least one adult who can share it, rediscovering with him the joy, excitement and mystery of the world we live in. Exploring nature with your children is largely a matter of becoming receptive to what lies all around you. It is learning again to use your eyes, ears, nostrils and finger tips.

In Part Two of this book there are four chapters, one for each season of the year. Each chapter in this section offers ideas of how adults can become tuned in to what is around them, whether out in a street, school grounds, a garden or on a walk. There are lists of things to look out for in each place and season, followed by suggestions for possible conversations to have with the children. Each chapter then offers lists of further resources that may be helpful in extending the children's experience in a variety of ways, including stories, art, music and websites.

Being outdoors with children on a daily basis means that we need to be resilient and flexible, in order to make an appropriate response to both the seasons and the weather. There is a growing awareness of global warming and the effect this is having on climate change. There is now no guarantee that snow falls in winter and the summer is hot and dry. Children need to be involved with the natural elements throughout the year as part of their interaction with the natural world.

Part Three, therefore, details the additional experiences offered by the four elements of earth, air, fire and water. It explains the importance of being connected in a physical and emotional way with these. Each chapter describes ways in which children can become involved in discovering and playing using either one or a combination of elements. Playing with mud, earth and sand is recognised as having prime importance in childhood and there are ideas of how to develop this play in early years settings. Similarly, going out in the rain is a valid experience in itself but there are also details and ideas for using rain to extend creativity and exploration. Being outside in wind, fog, snow and ice are all included in this section, as is a chapter considering how to offer a safe fire experience. There are lists of further resources at the end of each of the four chapters so that you can be prepared and are able to offer exciting learning opportunities whatever the weather or season.

The book concludes by emphasising the importance of offering children first-hand experiences of the natural world. The word 'experience' is used throughout the book in preference to the word 'activity'. This implies that adults and children should be sharing an experience at a deeper level rather than adults just providing an activity for children to do. It is important for children to experience for themselves the changing nature of the world around them. They cannot learn about the seasons purely from pictures, worksheets or photographs. They need to be able to use all their senses and have a rich first-hand experience so they really understand what is going on around them. Free play, exploration and child-initiated learning are of particular importance, and the characteristics of effective early learning, as outlined in the EYFS document, sit well with the way children learn outdoors.

This book is written for all adults who are involved with young children, whether at home or in an early years setting. It aims to introduce or rekindle some of our childhood experiences and encourage the adults, whether parents, grandparents or practitioners to develop a deeper awareness, appreciation and enthusiasm for what is happening around them outside. It may be something as simple as standing listening to raindrops pattering on a roof or a tree, or watching white clouds scudding along against a backdrop of brilliant blue. It may mean overcoming our own inhibitions about what were once termed 'creepy crawlies' but have gained elevated status as minibeasts, which are a continual source of fascination for young children. We need to understand the importance of children becoming deeply involved in play experiences, whether climbing a tree, splashing in a puddle or exploring a muddy space. Once we are able to feel comfortable within ourselves, we can then inspire, encourage and involve our children. If children have positive experiences and interactions with the natural world in their first five years it is likely that this will influence their attitudes and dispositions in adult life.

If we are able to pass onto the children in our care, an awareness, respect and love for the natural world, we will hopefully awake a desire in them to respond appropriately to issues of conservation and ecological sustainability on a global level as they become older. More importantly, however, we are offering the benefits, the joy and the fun of an outdoor childhood.

Part 1 — Outdoor learning and the Early Years Foundation Stage

This part of the book refers directly to the revised Early Years Foundation Stage (EYFS). The four chapters that follow show how close collaboration and an understanding of the way in which children learn will ensure that high-quality outdoor provision becomes a fully integrated part of the EYFS. Initially, practitioners need to understand how children learn effectively and then work together with colleagues, parents and children to plan and implement changes in the outdoor environment. These need to take into account the specific needs of your children as well as differing weather conditions and seasonal change. Adults now need to observe and assess children's progress in three prime areas of learning and four specific areas. Chapter 3 deals specifically with each of these areas in relation to the outdoors and suggests ways of developing appropriate learning opportunities. If children are really going to benefit from as much time outside as possible it is essential to work closely with parents and Chapter 4 suggest ways to do this.

Characteristics of effective learning

Introduction

In the statutory framework EYFS, paragraph 1.10 gives us the three main characteristics of effective learning: 'Playing and Exploring', 'Active Learning' and 'Creating and Thinking Critically'. There are three additional subheadings in each section outlining the different ways children learn. There is now a requirement for practitioners to reflect on these in their practice. This emphasises the focus on the importance of the learning process itself. There is a still a strong focus on play and discovery as the most important way in which children learn. There is, however, more awareness based on recent research that children need to be able to self-regulate their own learning. This is a concept that involves 'attitudes and dispositions for learning and an ability to be aware of one's own thinking. It also includes managing feelings and behaviour' (Tickell 2011: 87). There is a requirement for practitioners to observe the different ways in which children are learning and to foster ways to develop this.

This chapter looks at the ways in which the outdoors can be used to promote effective learning, using these headings. The ways in which children learn should, in turn, inform our thinking and planning, as we design our spaces and work with our children in them. An inspirational outdoor space, whether it is one you have created, or one you are able to access on a regular basis, can offer high-quality experiences throughout the year to enable children to learn effectively from an early age.

It is important when working within the EYFS to remember that the early learning goals are the expectations for children who are at the end of the Foundation Stage. Most children will transfer from a nursery preschool or childminder into a reception class in a primary school before the end of the Foundation Stage. We need to ensure that all children, whether at home or in early years settings, are working towards these goals, but it is even more important to ensure that they are establishing the patterns and styles of learning that will remain with them for life. Effective practice will enable children to develop attitudes and dispositions to manage their own feelings, behaviours and learning.

How children learn

Through play and discovery, young children are able to manage their own learning, thus developing lifelong skills. From the moment they are born, babies begin the learning process. Their behaviour is reinforced by experiences. A tiny baby only a few days old is able to copy the lip and mouth movements of adults. This usually sparks an emotional response in the adult, which is communicated back, and so the baby engages in social and emotional interaction. The learning process in a young baby is a complex interaction of instinctive, intuitive and learnt behaviours.

As parents, grandparents and practitioners, we all want the children in our care to become effective learners. In particular, children with additional needs may need more specific support and guidance so they, too, can learn effectively. Learning is not a passive process of knowledge acquisition with measurable and predictable outcomes. It is a process that draws on past experiences so the learner can understand and evaluate the present before taking action to shape the future and thereby acquire new knowledge. Adults play an important part in this learning process and need to understand how the learning process can best be developed. Vygotsky (1978) used the term 'scaffolding of learning' and explained how new learning takes place when supported by what has happened previously. He also introduced the term 'zone of proximal development' and this is where adult interaction can be most successful. It represents the gap between what the child already knows and what he or she is capable of learning with assistance from an adult or more knowledgeable and skilled peer.

The role of the outdoor space

Being outdoors will enable children and adults to have more freedom. Adults should be able to find time to observe the ways in which children are interacting with the environment and how their learning is being extended in different ways, according to the situation and also the different times of the year and the elements available. A skilled adult will be able to adapt and extend the natural environment to offer a wide range of learning experiences throughout the year.

Babies listen closely to sounds, and the development of internal language starts at a very young age. Sensory experiences are particularly important for very young children and babies respond immediately to the outdoor environment, watching movements, discovering textures and hearing new sounds. The focus of all provision should be the process of learning that is taking place in each child. Good outdoor provision does not necessarily rely on expensive equipment. It entails making the most of the natural spaces and resources you have, and combining this with positive, engaged and enthusiastic adults. Children's learning is a result of complex interactions between the child's experiences of relationships and environments. The following section looks specifically at the outdoors and how it can be used to create meaningful and enjoyable learning experiences for young children under the headings given as the characteristics of effective learning.

Playing and exploring

Children learn from direct involvement with the natural elements. As they explore sand, water, rain and snow, they become deeply involved, very often to the extent of being unaware of whatever else is going on around them. This connection is instinctive and seems to be part of our primeval need to remain in contact with the earth and what it offers us. Current research is now focusing on how this can help with emotional balance and also healing of body and mind. Sensory or experiential learning can be encouraged by adults who are able to appreciate and enjoy the experiences themselves. We may remember, as children, throwing leaves in the air just for fun, splashing in puddles and rolling down a hill. We need to encourage our children to engage in these childhood experiences.

Finding out and exploring

Babies and toddlers are keen to explore from the moment they are born. They often use their mouths to explore objects before they develop exploratory skills with hands and fingers. Outdoors they need access to a space that is exciting and challenging, but above all is safe. Small objects, pebbles and small stones need to be avoided, but it is important to offer different textures and surfaces for them to crawl and walk on. Toddlers enjoy the challenge of walking on a rough surface and show great concentration as they try to walk on uneven ground.

Karen Malone and Paul Tranter (2003) suggest that a play area that can be changed and modified provides more opportunities for environmental learning with corresponding behavioural consequences. Moore and Wong (1997) look at different aspects of play and how nature is important for children to develop properly through play. They assert that the type of place where children play has a direct influence on the quality of play.

In *Play Naturally* (Lester and Maudsley 2006), a review commissioned by the Children's Play Council, there is strong reaffirmation of the essential nature of play in childhood development. Children prefer natural environments to play in as they help to develop all types of play. There is also evidence that a natural setting can reduce bullying. Vegetation and other natural features can create enclosed areas to help different groups play together with a wider range of activities leading to better overall concentration and motor skills.

Using what they know in their play

Older children need access to a variety of resources outdoors to encourage them to play at a deeper level and develop their imaginations. Small hidey holes for babies will become the starting point for the sophisticated shelters designed and built by four and five-year-olds. Play involves doing, exploring, discovering, failing and succeeding. Children create and then recreate their own worlds using the knowledge gained from previous play. As you work with the children in your outdoor space you may be able to extend the challenges and opportunities simply by making more natural elements available to them.

Being willing to have a go

Encourage safe risk-taking and offer new experiences. A tree trunk needs to be climbed; log stepping stones are for jumping; a small wildlife pond waits to be explored. Provide real garden tools for children to work the soil, to dig, to plant and to weed, as they grow their own crops and flowers. There will be failures when some plants do not do as well as others, but children will discuss this with adults and each other and learn from this experience.

Active learning

Children will make direct connections with the natural environment as they find small creatures, observe leaves changing colour, and plant and grow their own crops. They will acquire new knowledge and use this to inform decision-making, even maybe as adults themselves in later life, working towards sustainability and planet awareness. Parents and practitioners have an important role as they give children the knowledge base they need to make informed judgements and decisions. Active learning should be supported when necessary through sensitive intervention to extend and deepen learning.

Being involved and concentrating

Children seem to respond naturally to the outdoor environment and it is important to ensure that there are additional resources to extend the play. A muddy puddle and a stick will enable a lively toddler to become deeply involved and become totally absorbed in this world. Older children, too, become absorbed in their play with natural elements of sand, mud and water. Research by Ferre Laevers et al. (2005) links the capacity of young children to become deeply involved in an activity with a state of well-being and increased levels of self-esteem.

Active learning will help to develop concentration as this child becomes totally absorbed with his stick and muddy puddle.

In a report written for the RSPB (2007), Dr William Bird outlines the research that suggests that children who have been diagnosed with ADHD will benefit from more time spent in the outdoors and, in particular, in green spaces. The research asserts that children are far more able to concentrate, focus and pay attention after being outside. The authors feel that as a general principle the nature-attention relationship will apply to all children. They suggest that all children's attentional functioning might benefit from incorporating vegetation into places where children live and play. As you plan your outdoor space bear this in mind. The benefits of being surrounded by plants and trees cannot be over-estimated.

Keeping on trying

The ability to persevere is one that we need to secure if we are going to succeed in adult life. As we watch a baby trying to crawl or reach out for an object beyond his grasp, it becomes evident that this characteristic of effective learning is present from a very early age. If children are allowed to play in a natural space from an early age, they will overcome the difficulties of walking through long grass, avoiding brambles and set themselves challenges as they climb trees or build dens. (See Case study: Walking through woods in autumn, Chapter 7, page 94–6.)

Enjoying achieving what they set out to do

This aspect reaches out across the curriculum. It may mean creating an artwork from natural materials. For a young toddler it may mean reaching the top of a tree stump, or for an older child climbing to a higher branch in a tree. It could be setting up a water system either in sand or mud, or using tubes and gutters and watching the first trickle flowing. A longer-term achievement comes when children are able to harvest and eat fruits and vegetables they have grown themselves.

Creating and thinking critically

From a very young age, children begin to follow their own desires, interests and instincts, and a supportive adult will extend this by interaction and also by providing appropriate resources. Children outdoors will create and recreate their own spaces and their own worlds and games, which as they get older involve complex systems of rules and order. They will learn to fail, to try again, to succeed and improve on their own inventions.

Children used crates and gutters to invent a water system, then experimented with gradient to see when the water would push small twigs down the gutters.

Having their own ideas

Children need to find their own challenges and then use their critical thinking skills to set their boundaries and targets. Rule-making, codes and passwords become an important part of the sophisticated play of older children and have their basis in the play systems established in the early years. Establish rich play opportunities with the basic materials of sand, mud and water (see following chapters) and talk and listen to children as they play. Providing flower petals, cones, pebbles, bark and leaves encourages creativity and allows children the freedom to discover the rules of pattern-making and design.

Noren-Bjorn (1982) describes how one girl throws a stone in a puddle and watches it make ripples. Another child joins her and tries to hit a 'target 'in the water. The girl begins to keep a score of how many times they hit it and then they move on to discuss what counts, thus setting their own rules and parameters.

Using what they already know to learn new things

Children will benefit from an environment where they can control the space, explore and experiment, destroy and rebuild. Outdoors, they can influence their surroundings and also begin to take responsibility for them. They need space for 'being' as well as 'doing'. Offer resources that will help them build their own spaces and encourage their problem-solving skills. It is possible to create a den even on a hard safety surface. Provide cones and stable supports, maybe an A-frame, hooks in fences or on walls, and offer a variety of covers and natural materials for children to create their private space. If the den needs to be packed away each day the children will become more adept each day at setting it up.

The benefits of growing crops and flowers with young children are huge. If children are in the same setting for more than a year they will be able to use experiences from the previous year and build on these in successive seasons. Hopefully these opportunities will be offered again several times during their school life.

Choosing ways to do things and finding new ways

Children need to be encouraged to talk about how they reach conclusions or solve problems. They are beginning to understand the nature of creative problem-solving. They will learn to ask questions about the world around them. They will observe the nature of change through the seasons and begin to understand the passing of time.

An important part of learning is the ability to use what you already know, but also to transfer it to a totally new experience and context. This is evident in the case study below when children visited an art gallery and used their knowledge in the creation of their own work using natural materials.

Case study

Encouraging creativity and creative thinking

A group of children from Bayonne Nursery visited the Courtauld Gallery at Somerset House. They were encouraged to 'be joyous and comment on shape and space, to explore spaces, to sit, be peaceful and think about the works in front of them'. They chose postcards of their favourite pictures. On return to the nursery children drew their own pictures based on their previous learning experiences at the gallery. They spoke about what they had seen. Ben said he could see squares, triangles, straight lines and zigzags in a rug weaving. Manuel liked the Monet picture and he noticed the mountains in the background and the waves in the sea. Ben liked the Monet, too, and produced his own picture, added a boat, a swimmer and lots of rain (there had been a very wet spell of weather). Olivia spent time looking at Pablo Picasso's picture of a child looking at a bird.

During the next few days children went out on a forest school trip and came back with lots of very tiny leaves they had collected. They wanted to make pictures and mixed brown paint with the glue. One child who had visited the art gallery said, 'We must make frames, like the ones we saw'. Children used string and small sticks to turn their creations into wall hangings. Another area of learning was explored as children measured, balanced and cut twigs and string.

In this example we can see how incidental learning is transferred to another experience as children absorb knowledge and then use it in another way. The framing idea was a direct result of their visit to the art gallery. Frames did not seem to be something the children had commented on while at the gallery but obviously had made an impression.

Children need to be exposed to a range of natural and creative experiences if they are to develop their ability to create and think critically. Children can be encouraged to interact with the natural environment and be offered the chance to see how other children and adults have responded to the world around them. Visits to museums and galleries should be arranged whenever possible, or it may be that a visiting artist or musician can come to the setting and work with the children to explore music and art. Introducing works of art through books, pictures and videos can also support children's interests.

Conclusion

The innate curiosity of a tiny baby needs stimulus if it is to develop and become confident to explore the environment around. With sensitive adult interaction, children hear language and begin to develop their own thought processes and their self-confidence. They begin to have ideas of their own and manipulate the world around them to extend their interest and involvement. Rich sensory experiences need to be combined with an understanding that children need space and uninterrupted time to become deeply involved in the learning process. Outdoor learning experiences are often remembered for a lifetime. Play is at the heart of it all; whether it takes place in your own garden or further afield. It adds relevance and depth to the curriculum in ways that are difficult or impossible to achieve indoors.

At heart, all learning is about going from what is known and familiar to what is unknown and uncertain. So learning, growth and development depends upon risk. Outdoor environments offer the best opportunities for children to get to grips with the unpredictable, engaging, challenging world around them.

(Quoted in Community Playthings 2007: 19)

2 | Creating an enabling environment outdoors – design, layout and planting

Designing your outdoor space

However small your outdoor space, it is important to evaluate on a regular basis how children are using it and think about any ways you can improve the nature of the experiences you are offering outdoors throughout the year. A challenging outdoor space will offer opportunities for children to experience something of the natural world and involve themselves in a range of play opportunities using both natural and man-made materials.

The three characteristics of effective learning as defined in the EYFS, challenge us, as practitioners, to make the most of our outdoor spaces to allow children to discover and explore, become deeply involved in active learning, develop their self-confidence, and be able to create and think critically.

We need to provide an enabling environment that is carefully designed to meet the needs of the children in our care. Some settings will need to consider how to provide for very young children, and in any layout it is important to consider how all children can access the environment we offer, even if they are not fully mobile.

There are still some settings that have no access to their own space but need to take children to a local park or a nearby school's playing field. Looking carefully at that provision within the context of this book will hopefully allow children to have a wider range of learning experiences throughout the year.

Recent years have seen the growth of forest schools and the importance of letting children play in natural environments. Many settings are now beginning to take children out to nearby woodland or park space, even if it is only for a few sessions. Most local authorities have heard about forest schools and many more practitioners are attending training.

Outdoor spaces in early years settings may range from a shared, small piece of tarmac in a community or church hall, to larger spaces of mixed hard and soft surfaces, to some settings that have direct access to their own wild natural spaces, such as fields and woodlands.

Getting started

The first consideration is to look at your existing space and see how you can maximise the impact of the natural world. It should involve listening to children and trying to understand how they use existing spaces and encouraging them to talk about the nature of their play. You should also involve parents and at a later stage maybe a garden designer or architect. If you do this, it is important to find someone who understands what opportunities and experiences you want to offer your children.

It may involve planting or creating spaces for play on a larger scale with natural materials. It may mean importing some logs or a small tree trunk, making a pond or providing a space to grow vegetables. You may be able to plant some more herbs to attract bees and butterflies or find a dip in the ground where you can make a puddle for children to play in.

As you consider your current outdoor provision think about whether children are able to:

- observe wildlife, birds, minibeasts, frogs, tadpoles and insects
- plant crops and flowers
- find places to relax and be quiet
- sit quietly either with a book or some music
- use a range of natural and man-made materials to create their own scenarios
- become deeply involved in playing with natural materials such as sand, mud and water
- dig and explore the ground
- run, shout and climb
- find a space where they can make patterns or pictures using natural materials such as flower petals and seed heads
- recreate in a variety of ways the experiences of the natural world around them
- use their imaginations and ingenuity to invent and extend their own play.

Work together as a team and make a list of the experiences you would like to offer your children. Look at your space and then, working together to include parents and children, discuss how you can make the very best of the space that you have and how you can transform it into an environment that offers excitement, challenge and change through the year.

All settings should consider the basic provision of sand and water, and how they can offer this outside in ways that will offer a different experience from indoor provision. A space to grow vegetables should be in a sunny position, if possible, and could be a plot or raised bed. Vegetables can be grown in large containers if you have very little space. Think, too, about how you can provide natural spaces and make places where children can hide away. Good storage for outdoor equipment is essential and should be made as accessible as possible.

Sand play

A sandpit that is large enough for children to climb into is a must if you have the space. There is an on-going argument as to whether it needs to be covered and if so what type of cover is best. Everyone needs to work this out for themselves. Sand can be used through the year, not just in the summer. If the sandpit is situated under a tree it will benefit from having a cover to protect it from leaf drop in the autumn. Before installing a sandpit, think about the position of the sun and whether it may become too hot in the summer. Can you provide sufficient shade?

If the sandpit can be sunk into the ground, it can slope down towards the back, giving opportunities for much deeper digging. Children can become involved in beach-type play, making holes, sandcastles and sculptures. Having the top of the sand at the same level as the surrounding surface makes it easy to sweep the sand back into the pit at the end of a session. A large, open sandpit can often be used together with water at any time of the year. This is particularly popular in the summer to offer a beach experience.

If you have limited or shared outdoor space, try to offer more than one sand tray so children can use wet or dry sand. A small table or wooden board placed nearby encourages more sophisticated play as children can fill and empty containers and begin to develop imaginative play. Very young children will love to explore the sand and if you have a wide age range it may mean that two trays are better than one!

Water play

Many settings use a shallow plastic water tray filled with a few inches of water and a variety of jugs and plastic toys. Outdoor water play offers the chance to be more adventurous. Think about providing a deeper container, maybe a zinc bath where children can feel the depth and volume of water. Provide a source they can access themselves. This could be a camping water carrier or a water butt where they can fill watering cans to water the garden. Encourage children to think about conserving water. They can help to empty the water tray using watering cans to water any surrounding plants. Provide additional resources such as planks, pipes and gutters, with nearby storage so children can use these in a variety of ways as they wish. Sticky duct tape enables lengths of piping to be fixed anywhere as children learn about siphoning and pressure. As water is a natural resource children will enjoy playing with it in its natural form. Rain play, puddle play and mud play are experiences which are easy to provide if children and adults are dressed appropriately.

Den play

There should be provision for children of all ages to build and play in dens and shelters throughout the year. Small pack-away tents make safe places for very young children and can be used in shared spaces. It is more challenging, however, for children to make their own dens. Providing a resource box (see list of further resources on page 27) and making seasonal variations will enable them to be more creative and solve problems as they work together to build their den. If you have a larger space, try to provide some tree branches or foliage such as bracken, which can be made into a shelter. Raised platforms often make a good space. A hook in a wall and a line attached to a post will give the basis for suspending a fabric cover to make a simple shelter. Nearby natural resources that children have collected will enhance the play. Think about storage for these as you design your space.

Spaces for movement

Children need space to run, jump and climb. Research has shown that fixed climbing structures offer little challenge once they have been used a few times. They are also

This tree presents more challenges than a climbing frame and is used by these children every day.

expensive and take up a lot of space. If you have any natural features such as logs or trees, they can be used to encourage physical activity in children of all ages. You will need to make a risk-benefit assessment and check that there are no features that are likely to cause injury such as sharp twigs sticking out at an angle. Plan, too, to leave some free space for children to use in different ways.

Natural spaces

This term can be used loosely to describe a space where the animals and plants are given priority. It may be a pile of logs, a quiet space surrounded by tall plants, a small pond, or a flower bed planted to attract a range of insects and pollinators. If you have a larger outdoor space, there can be grassy meadows, or some trees planted to give a sheltered circle for children to come together to play. Bushes to hide in and tree trunks to climb offer the very best experiences for children.

Storage

Storage needs to be one of the first considerations in any development project. It needs to be accessible for children. Items need to be clearly labelled and well organised so children can put them away easily.

If you have to pack away every day, small trolleys and wheeled storage units are essential. If you have your own space it is worth investing in improving boundaries to make the site secure. It is then often possible to leave plastic storage containers outside permanently. Garden tools need to be carefully stored. In a pack-away setting, a small trolley with baskets might offer a solution. Alternatively, they can be stored on a picture board which has the outline of each tool and a suitable hook to hang it on. Children need to learn about the need to use tools safely and also how to look after them.

Planting your outdoor space

Once you have the basic layout of your space and have decided where to place permanent fixtures such as a sandpit, a quiet area, maybe a wildlife space with a small pond and logs, you will need to think about planting. Try to choose plants, trees and shrubs that offer interest at different times of the year and those which will provide a natural source of play material. With careful planning, it is possible to have colour, shape, texture and form throughout the year, even in a very small space. If you have a shared space, planting in raised beds or containers may be the only way you can do this. Even tubs and containers can provide seasonal interest and can be moved around in smaller spaces to mark out different areas or to create boundaries.

Suggestions for container planting for small or shared spaces
Spring interest

Plant containers up in the autumn and make sure that they are in a sheltered space. In frosty weather it is a good idea to cover them with garden fleece or layers of bracken and bubble wrap. A variety of spring bulbs – daffodils, tulips, small crocus –can all be packed fairly tightly into one container with good soil or planting compost. *Corylus contorta*, or twisted willow, in a larger pot will give catkins and this can be pruned when necessary. Children will enjoy using the catkins in their play. Try underplanting with native primroses for a really spring-like feel. These can now be bought from most good garden centres and can be divided each year to produce more plants.

Summer interest

Pots of lavender and herbs will attract butterflies as well as a range of other small insects. *Verbena rigida* is easy to grow from seed and has a long flowering season. This deep purple plant is a food source for many species. Pots will need daily watering in hot, sunny weather.

Summer-flowering bulbs can be planted between October and February and will give additional colour and perfume. Lilies are strongly perfumed but beware of brushing against the pollen as it can stain clothing.

Sweet peas can be grown in containers as long as there is a minimum soil depth of 8 inches. They need support and ideally should be trained against a nearby fence or wall. If you need to put a support in the pot, the pot should be large enough to hold this. Sweet pea seeds should not be eaten and extra care must be taken if children are helping to plant these. The plants, however, provide scented flowers that children can cut and arrange themselves. The more the flowers are cut the more they produce.

A range of vegetables can be grown in containers and children can help to plant seeds or buy small plug plants in the spring. Combine lettuce with a beetroot plant and some parsley. Trailing tomatoes will grow in a container and need to be well watered. Strawberries can be grown in an ordinary pot or a special strawberry planter. They need lots of water!

Autumn interest

A small acer (Japanese maple) will do well in a container if it is planted in ericaceous compost. It will need some frost protection during winter months. Wrap bubble wrap round the pot and secure with string or tape. From September onwards, it will give rich shades and when the leaves finally drop, children can use the attractive shapes in creative play. It will need to be re-potted every two or three years to give the roots fresh compost and more space.

Flowers, vegetables and herbs can all be grown successfully in containers and children enjoy watering them.

Create a mini orchard in a container. Fill a 50-centimetre pot with good compost and plant a dwarf apple tree. If you have space, try a pear or plum tree grafted onto dwarfing rootstock.

Winter interest

Heathers and dwarf conifers will give colour and texture through the winter months. Put some crocuses in the same pot and they will push through in January. A small tree such as *magnolia stellata* can be planted in a container together with snowdrops, spring bulbs and, lower down in the pot, some summer-flowering lilies. The snowdrops will appear first, followed by any other spring bulbs. In late March, the magnolia should flower. Once the delicate white magnolia flowers have finished, the lilies will take over and add interest through the late spring and summer.

Bamboo grown in pots gives a versatile resource. It adds greenery to spaces in the winter as well as year round, and can be used to make secret places, tunnels and arches. Grasses can also be grown in pots or small beds. The flowers seeds and stems can be cut and used by children in their play.

Planting in larger spaces

In a larger space you may have room to include a greater variety of plants. Think about different heights and how plants can be used to divide different areas. Think, too, about how some can be used to create secret spaces, nooks and crannies where children can enter into their own secret world of imaginative play.

Spring interest

BULBS

- Daffodils and narcissus: plant in a range of sizes and colours.
- Muscari or grape hyacinth: easy to grow and will spread. Children can cut these and use them to decorate dens or make flower arrangements for use indoors.
- Hyacinths: these can also be grown in a glass container so children can see the root growth.
- Bluebells: these are suitable for planting in a wild space but tend to spread in a small garden.
- Tulips: a range of bright colours will brighten up any space. Sometimes it is easier to plant them in deep pots and place the pots in different places around your garden.

FLOWERS

Native primroses (*primula vulgaris*) can be obtained from most garden centres. There are many varieties of coloured primulas or primroses, which can be used to brighten up a dark corner or container.

SHRUBS

Twisted hazel, or *corylus contorta*, provides interesting winter twig shapes and catkins in the spring. Camellias are a good evergreen bush with beautiful flowers that drop petals, which can be used in play. They are, however, susceptible to frost damage and need to be planted in a sheltered spot away from early morning sunlight.

TREES

Ornamental cherry trees or a fruit tree such as apple or pear will give a plentiful supply of spring blossom for children to play with. Larch trees come out in spring and give attractive bright green foliage. A weeping larch such as *larix kaempferi*, 'Blue Rabbit', will eventually make a shady hiding space for children as well as providing a supply of small twigs and cones for play.

Summer interest

BULBS

Lilies and nerines are the most suitable summer bulbs for a nursery and can be grown in containers.

FLOWERS

A range of plants to attract wildlife is the best choice and some can be grown from seed. Others can be bought as small plants and children can help to plant them out. Scabious and *verbena bonariensis* can be grown from seed. Children enjoy planting and growing sunflowers, and even very young children will be able to put a sunflower seed in a pot. Mini sunflowers, 'Teddy Bear', produce pom-pom heads, which are good for imaginative play. *Nigella* is very easy to grow from seed. It gives pretty pale blue flowers and then wonderful shaped seed heads, which can be picked and dried for use in a collection of natural play materials.

SHRUBS

Photinia fraserii, or 'Red Robin', is an easy-to-grow shrub that gives bright red foliage in late spring and summer as new leaves and shoots develop. It is good for screening and can be easily pruned if it gets too large. Weigela is a group of shrubs that bears brightly coloured flowers to add colour to any bed. Buddleias are hardy shrubs that can grow quickly and become quite large. They produce long plume-like flowers that attract a range of butterflies and insects. As the flowers die back, they can be pruned for use by children in their play. Cornus are a group of shrubs, some of which can be pruned hard in summer to give coloured stems in the winter. Cornus alba is the most common and produces red twigs in winter when hard pruned. In the summer it has flattened heads of star-shaped, creamy-white flowers, good for adding to imaginary perfumes and potions.

TREES

Many of our native trees come into full flower in early summer and provide leaves, twigs and fruits at different times of the year. Oak, ash and chestnut are all large trees and only thrive in larger spaces. If you have a smaller space, you may be able to plant some silver birch trees and prune them regularly if they get too large. They provide a shimmering canopy of leaves that rustle in the breeze as well as an attractive shiny bark. *Cornus variegata* is a deciduous tree with layered branches and attractive pinky-cream and green leaves.

Autumn interest

BULBS

Autumn crocus will flower from September and flourish in natural spaces under trees.

FLOWERS

Sunflowers can be grown from seed by the children. Start them in the spring and by autumn the plants should have reached full height and will liven up any dark corner. Different varieties give different heights.

SHRUBS

Cotinus Coggyria 'Flame', commonly known as the smoke bush, has deep purple, round leaves, which change to an even deeper colour in the autumn. *Rhus typhina*, commonly known as 'Stag's horn sumach', can get quite large and can spread by underground suckers. It has bright orange and red leaves in autumn.

TREES

Acers are a group of trees that are suitable for small spaces and provide wonderful autumn shade. Different varieties have different leaf shapes but all are attractive and can be used by children in play.

Winter interest

BULBS

Snowdrops and crocus need to be planted in late spring for them to flower well the following winter.

FLOWERS

There are few plants that flower in the winter, but many shrubs bear fruit and flowers during the winter months. Witch hazel flowers appear from January onwards. There are several varieties suitable for small spaces, but these shrubs do better if sheltered from strong winds. *Hamamelis mollis* (Chinese witch hazel) produces bright yellow flowers with a strong fragrance on bare branches in late winter. *Viburnum bodnantense*, 'Dawn', is a scented, winter-flowering shrub with pretty pink flowers from November to March.

SHRUBS

Garrya elliptica is a useful evergreen shrub. It grows fairly quickly and is good for screening. It also has long, green catkins that children can use in play in the winter.

Pyracantha and hawthorn hedges will provide food for birds through the winter, but are very sharp and should only be planted where children cannot reach them.

TREES

By planting some evergreen trees you can provide winter interest. Conifers will provide cones for children in play and there are many smaller or dwarf varieties available.

Conclusion

When planning to make changes, it is important to spend time researching ideas. Talk to parents and children. Visit other settings that have worked on this process. Find out what went well and what they might now do differently. Above all, make time to share with each other your vision and ideas of the outdoor experiences you want children to have through the year, and plan carefully how you can achieve at least some of these.

Further resources

Every Nursery Needs a Garden by Ann Watts (Routledge 2011).
A comprehensive list of ideas for developing outdoor spaces, with guidance for initiating and sustaining a project to offer high-quality provision. There are details for planting flowers and vegetables through the year and lists of suitable plants for nursery spaces.

Gardening with Children by Kim Wilde (Collins 2007).
Plant it: A Step by Step Guide to Creating a Beautiful Garden by J. Edwards (Anness 2002).
Playing Outdoors: Spaces and Places, Risk and Challenge by Helen Tovey (Oxford University Press 2007).

Website resources

Learning through Landscapes website: www.ltl.org.uk/resources
Go to Resources and select 'training advice sheets' and 'early years'. Download 'Advice on sand in your grounds' and 'Den building'. Also useful are 'The art of the sandpit' and 'Small spaces, big experiences', which are available for download to members.

Creating an enabling environment outdoors – areas of learning

3

As you consider how to improve your outdoor space, it is important to hold in your mind the characteristics of effective learning and see how the space can be adapted to provide the best possible learning opportunities throughout the year. This section focuses on each area of the curriculum in turn and outlines additional resources and experiences you can offer to ensure that each of the areas is covered.

It is crucial, however, to remember that the best learning and play opportunities will cover many areas of the curriculum at the same time. These areas are closely interwoven and children benefit from a holistic learning experience which encompasses these. In particular, the three prime areas of learning are interdependent and their strands are like the threads of a textured, woven pattern and come together to create a whole.

Personal, social and emotional development

> The natural world provides the major stimulus and most significant context for emotional experience with its ever changing and diverse scenes offering the widest range of possible interactions.
>
> (Moore 1997)

If we are to introduce children to these experiences it is imperative that we are able to acquaint ourselves in some way with the world of nature. It may mean going back to our own childhood and thinking about experiences we still recall with pleasure. We may need to become more familiar with the animals and plants around us and for some, this may mean taking on a healthier lifestyle as we spend more time in the open air and imbibe something of the world around us.

Making relationships

Establishing close relationships with the children in our care means that there is mutual trust, and shared outdoor experiences will help to build and consolidate these relationships.

Adults need to be able to share a child's excitement at seeing a butterfly, or finding a frog, as well as encouraging a child who may be afraid of small insects. Children, too, will help each other as in the case of four-year-old Harry, who carefully explained to his two-year-old sister who was nervous of flying insects, 'A butterfly is very pretty, it just flies around and it would never hurt you'.

Additional resources and experiences

- Opportunities to join in group gardening activities, and care for plants and wildlife.
- Provision of crates, blocks, tyres etc. will encourage group play and social interaction.

Self-confidence and self-awareness

As children develop understanding of the ways in which the seasons affect the habits and growth of plants and animals, they will develop the self-awareness and the belief that they can be involved in these processes. Just encouraging a shy child to join in with a group planting potatoes is a good way to encourage this state of emotional well-being and develop self-confidence.

Additional resources and experiences

- Challenging physical experiences that will encourage their self-confidence, e.g. a tree trunk lying on its side, stepping stone logs, or rocks to clamber on.
- Muddy puddles – watch very young children as they decide whether or not to risk stepping into the water and then experiencing joy and excitement as they splash around.
- Large-scale opportunities to become involved in deep-level engagement with sand, mud and water.

Managing feelings and behaviour

Many children are naturally excited simply at being outside and feelings of exuberance may predominate. However, as children spend more time outside in a stimulating natural environment they will have periods of calm and sometimes reflection. With the support of adults, they will learn to listen to the song of birds, hear grasses in the wind and develop an awareness of the life that is going on around them.

Some children may initially be nervous when they find and interact with small creatures. Some may want to destroy them and impulse control can be developed with support from peers and adults. Our twenty-month grandson was frightened of worms and though he had a limited vocabulary he said 'nake, nake' and obviously thought these were snakes and somehow had learnt that snakes were creatures that evoked fear. It took some weeks before he was sufficiently reassured to watch them calmly.

Additional resources and experiences

- Establish rules that encourage care and respect for each other when outside, as well as for the plants and wildlife around them.
- Provide opportunities to care for wildlife by building and preserving habitats, feeding birds and growing flowers to attract bees.
- Teach children how to care for garden equipment and store it safely.

Physical development

Moving and handling

Children need to use their whole bodies to experience the world around them. Even older children still need to crawl, roll and lie down. They love being buried in sand, lying in water or rolling down a hill. A young baby can use all of its senses when it is taken outside.

Watching toddlers walk in woodland for the first time gives us a sense of deep emotion as we realise the way they are concentrating. Even though they have only just learnt to walk, they take extra care and meet the challenge of walking on uneven ground, negotiating twigs, sticks and long grass.

Two-year-olds in Reggio Emilia were given very large blocks of clay to explore as a whole body experience.

Additional resources and experiences

- Provide different textured surfaces for babies to crawl on or through, and tunnels of grass or moss, bark or woodland paths for toddlers to explore.
- Offer various loose parts – cardboard boxes and tubes, crates, building blocks of different shapes and sizes.
- Make natural building materials out of pieces of wood or tree branches cut to different sizes and thicknesses.

This baby is in the woods for the first time and is totally absorbed with his immediate environment.

- Stepping stone logs can be set up, but either they need to be covered in a wire mesh as they can get very slippery in wet weather or children need to be made aware of this and may decide not to use them.
- Look carefully at your space and see how you can adapt it through the year to offer different physical challenges by adding planks, a rope walkway or a fallen tree (landscapers or garden contractors may be willing to install one). Tree branches and logs are a natural climbing frame – complete a risk-benefit assessment and, if necessary, ask a forestry expert to inspect the tree.
- Provide collections of small objects such as conkers, pine needles, flower petals, grasses, dried flower heads, shells and cones to develop fine motor control.
- Encourage mixing potions with sticks or making 'paint' out of water and mud to paint a den. Large arm movements will help develop the finer movements needed for later pencil control and the outdoor spaces offer more opportunity for this. Boys, in particular, can become very involved in these experiences.
- Children will use natural materials such as sticks and twigs to make marks in sand and mud. Observe and discuss the shapes and patterns they can make.
- Encourage children to move in different ways after observing the movements they see outside – leaves falling, trees swaying, snowflakes floating, frogs hopping, worms wriggling etc.

Health and self-care

Developing a healthy lifestyle for all children is vitally important and our nation currently has high figures of obesity in young children. Being outdoors every day and exercising as much as possible is the first essential. Children need to be energetic, but also need to learn how their body responds to exercise and then to understand the need for rest and calm. Outdoor play needs to offer challenge and the opportunity for risk-taking. Children need to learn how to keep safe. A well-planned outdoor space will offer challenge and opportunity for physical activity as well as a space where plants are used to create a sense of calm and relaxation.

Additional resources and experiences

- Ensure babies are kept warm in winter and cool in summer. Provide outdoor sleeping places for babies, maybe under a tree.
- Help children to understand how to dress appropriately according to weather conditions. Provide boxes of appropriate clothing.
- Talk about different seasons and how plants and animals adapt. Discuss what we need to do differently to enable us to enjoy the different weather and seasons.
- Discuss why children need to wash hands after being outside and in particular if they have handled soil, plants or any creatures.
- Provide opportunities to grow, harvest and eat food.
- Discuss why we should eat fresh fruit and vegetables as opposed to sweets, biscuits and fried food.
- Offer food outdoors – hot soup in winter, iced fruit in summer. Plan picnics and maybe events where parents can join in. Children will often try new food in a different environment.
- Cook healthy meals – see recipes in Appendix (page 171–92).
- Provide a source of drinking water outside, particularly in hot weather.
- Provide a safe space where you can light a fire. Inform parents about why and when you plan to do this. Talk to children about safety and in particular the use of matches. Let them enjoy the sounds of crackling wood and the smell of wood smoke. Maybe you can cook something over the fire such as a pan of sausages or hot water for drinks.

Communication and language

Listening and attention

Young babies as well as older children will respond to outdoor sounds. By creating an environment of calm and drawing their attention to the gentle sounds of leaves in the wind or trickling water, we can help them to begin to focus their attention. This is a crucial element in the development of a child's ability to acquire language. Use rhymes and stories that relate to outdoor experiences and create special places where children can listen to stories.

Additional resources and experiences

- Provide wind chimes of different styles and materials. Very young children can hear a range of sounds and pitches.
- Give babies wooden instruments and shakers to make rain noises and rhythms.
- Give older children instruments to create quiet sounds and to imitate the natural sounds they hear in the environment. Make and use rain sticks.
- Draw attention to the different sounds in different seasons and weathers: rain pattering on the roof or hail on an umbrella; the silence of falling snow; rustling leaves in the breeze or the crisp crunch as you walk through them in the autumn.
- If you go out to a park or garden you may hear lawnmowers in the summer and leaf blowers in the autumn.
- Go for listening walks or have a time when you sit quietly with a small group and listen. Discuss the sounds you hear.
- Use a CD to distinguish different types of birdsong (available from the RSPB website or shop).
- Use rhymes and poems.

Understanding

Talking to babies from their very first day will accustom them to the sounds of language as well as develop an emotional response. Parents are the child's first educators and are usually responsible for the quality of the first language experiences of their children. Using small rhymes and interactive sounds in daily routines helps children to begin to understand the nature and meaning of words as well as becoming accustomed to the linguistic sound patterns of their home language.

Using natural materials to make small figures, these children were encouraged to retell the story of their outing to the woods, adding an imaginative ending to the tale.

Additional resources and experiences

- Photo cards of life cycles will help younger children or children with English as an additional language understand processes.
- Model how to do simple things such as digging a hole or sowing seeds, using words at the same time and repeating them.

Speaking

When outside with very young children, be aware of their response to the environment and use appropriate words. Listen to the sounds babies use and make up simple rhythmic responses. Build on existing vocabulary and use the correct names for artefacts and living things outdoors. Abstract concepts such as growth over time, the weather and the seasons will only be understood as children listen and then try to express their own ideas and thoughts. Children need to be given time to observe and listen before they speak.

Additional resources and experiences

- If your outdoor space has small, secluded areas, this will encourage children to talk to each other. Alternatively, if you do not have your own space, create small, cosy areas where children can just sit and chat to each other. Pots of flowers or bamboo can mark out boundaries and fabrics and covers can make shelters.

- Use puppets in a den or tent.
- Provide natural environments for small world play using rocks, stones, branches and cones. Dinosaurs, zoo and farm animals could be made available.

Literacy

Reading

Looking at books alone or sharing with a friend or an adult should be an enjoyable and comfortable experience. All children will need a variety of books to use outside every day.

Story tents or a rug under a large tree often give the sense of a special place where children will be able to concentrate on looking at books. In the winter, put books inside a den or tent. Provide rugs, sleeping bags or duvets outside so children can snuggle up warmly.

Additional resources and experiences

- Babies will enjoy looking at books outside from a very early age. Use bright clear pictures with very small children to help them relate their outdoor experiences to books.
- Laminated pictures of wildlife can be displayed outside and these should include words and pictures so children can identify creatures as they find them.
- Reference books should be easily available, so children know where they can identify their discoveries. They may have questions about the weather or the season and it is important that adults as well as children know where to find the answers.
- Outdoor role-play gives many opportunities for providing relevant texts.
- Make books about planting and growing, using photographs or children's drawings. Write simple sentences about each stage and read them back to children as they look at the books.
- Make simple booklets showing some of the different things children can discover in each season.
- Label seasonal collections of natural objects and provide another set of name cards so children can match them.

Writing

Children may begin to make marks outdoors from a very early age. Observe when they begin to give meaning to these marks.

Additional resources and experiences

- Try to find as many opportunities as possible to offer writing experiences outside. Role-play gives many opportunities for adults and children to write. Children can be encouraged to write their own lists, make tickets, write letters etc. (See the case study in Chapter 7, 'Winter', where children wrote letters to the giant.)

- Children can write their names in sand, mud or with small pebbles. Use a familiar story such as *Rosie's Walk* by Pat Hutchins, *We're Going on a Bear Hunt* by Michael Rosen or *The Gruffalo* by Julia Donaldson and help children to make signs for outdoor trails or tracks to follow the story line.

- A good supply of writing materials needs to be available outside and should include pens and pencils of different thicknesses as well as a variety of paper and card.

- Clip boards will ensure children can write in a variety of outdoor spaces as they wish.

- Model writing whenever possible in all role-play situations.

Mathematics

Numbers

Babies and young toddlers will begin to understand the concept of numbers as they move objects around. They love to fill containers. Provide a basket and large pine cones and use numbers to count as they put each one in the basket. As older children play with sand, water and mud, conversations will occur where you can use number language. If you supply small bun tins in the sand, children may discuss how many buns there are in a row. By looking at how many altogether, how many more do we need to fill the tin, how many have been eaten etc., they will begin to grasp the concept of multiplication, addition and subtraction.

Additional resources and experiences

- Vegetables can be planted in rows. Talk to children so they can see and begin to understand how the three rows of three tomatoes make a total of nine plants.

- Plant potatoes with children of all ages and talk to them about the number in the packet, how many are left, how many have been planted. Very young children learn about one-to-one correspondence as they plant one potato in each hole.

- Encourage children to record what they have planted using drawings, numbers or tally marks.

- Provide natural resources so children can work with larger amounts as they play, sharing out pebbles, fir cones, or small sticks for sausages.

- Harvest home-grown strawberries and share these out. They may need to be cut into sections and divided out between the children.

- Use number rhymes outside with children, and make up seasonal number rhymes, e.g. *Five yellow daffodils growing near the door / Louisa came and picked one and that left four / Four yellow daffodils growing near a tree* etc. Using children's names and real flowers helps children to focus and really understand how to count down. Change the words according to the season e.g. white snowdrops, summer roses, shiny blackberries.

Shape, space and measure

Young babies will use their whole bodies to explore space. Provide hidey holes, dens and spaces. Toddlers will love moving around and whole-body experiences of being in, on, under, below and above something or someone help to develop spatial awareness. Use the appropriate language as you interact with the children, so they begin to use the words 'in' and 'on', 'big' and 'little'.

Additional resources and experiences

- If you are redesigning your outdoor space, use layout plans with children and build their ideas into the plan.

- Encourage children to make trails, patterns and designs from natural materials.

- Autumn leaves can be sorted into baskets of big and little leaves.

- Compare sizes of conkers, arrange them in order, share them out or sort them into groups of similar sizes.

- Measure the height of plants as they grow. Sunflowers are one of the easiest plants to do this with. Help children to record the growth of plants using camera, tape measures or a graph using units, e.g. one child's hand length could be one square or large sticker on a graph. Why are some plants taller, shorter?

- Look at patterns that occur in nature such as concentric circles. Look at the rings in a tree trunk; maybe link them to ripples in a puddle as the child throws in a pebble. Compare this with Kandinsky's painting, 'Squares with Concentric Circles'. Find spirals on snail shells, spots on butterflies, stripes on flying insects and symmetry on leaves.

- Provide containers of different shapes and sizes in water and in dry and wet sand.

- Rain gauges or different containers can be used to measure rainfall.

- Any cooking activity will involve mathematical thinking and language. Children will cut fruit or vegetables, add eggs, mix and weigh out ingredients. They will be able to observe changes and share out the final feast.

- Children can learn to talk about money by setting up an outdoor shop for parents and friends. If you have any extra flowers, or crops, children could sell these to parents. Lavender can be picked in the summer and made into small bunches to sell for a few pence. Any surplus vegetables such as beans or tomatoes could be counted out into bags and sold.

Understanding the world

People and communities

As children grow older they will begin to develop awareness of other cultures and the community in which they live. One four-year-old was out in the woods where she had made a den. She was excited and said, 'This is a lovely house – all people can go in it – people from all over the world'.

Additional resources and experiences

- Planned walks can include visits to special places in your community at different times of the year.
- One nursery visits nearby allotments and children work with allotment holders. Another enters the local village show and children work hard to submit their entries.
- Festivals can be celebrated in the outdoor space. Use plants to make decorations for Christmas and Chinese New Year. Hang lanterns and lights outside for Diwali.
- Encourage all families to use the outdoor space as much as possible.

The world

Children should experience the natural world on a daily basis and adults should reinforce these interactions by discussion and reference. Using the weather and seasons as suggested in later chapters will offer children a resource that they will be able to draw on through later life.

Additional resources and experiences

- Encourage children to be aware of the changing seasons.
- Encourage an interest in the animals and birds that they observe. Feeding birds, building a small pond or making a log pile for insects are just a few of the ways that children learn to care for the natural world.
- Discuss how different parts of the world have different seasons and climates. Children from many countries may not experience snow or cold weather. Children

and families who arrive from other countries may need help to adjust to our climate as well as our culture and language.

- Provide books and stories outdoors showing foods grown in other countries, e.g. *Handa's Surprise* by Eileen Browne.

Technology

Digital cameras can be used at all times of the year to record events, patterns and sequences. Help children to select a few of their best photographs to print and maybe make into a book or display picture. Using a camera to record sequences of time and growth will provoke discussion and critical thinking. Children can take photographs of a sunset every few minutes and then arrange the printed pictures in the right sequence. Programmable toys can be used outdoors. Bee-Bot programmable robots are based on insect designs. Scanners and metal detectors can also be used outdoors. A light box can be used with great effect at all times of the year as children can collect and display natural materials giving more opportunity to explore colour, shape and texture.

If you have gained parental permission for children to access websites, try to direct them to some of the sites listed at the end of each section of this book to help them to identify living things, and to find out more about the world in which we live, its seasonal changes and weather patterns.

Additional resources and experiences

- ictearlyyears.e2bn.org is an excellent website with advice and ideas, including ways to use ICT outdoors.
- Consider buying a digital microscope, which can be used with a computer. They are expensive, but cheaper versions are becoming available.
- Chapter 5 details how a video camera was installed in a nest box so children can watch blue tits incubating and feeding their young.

Expressive arts and design

Exploring media and materials

The natural environment is a wonderful source of inspiration for artists. Dancers, painters, sculptors and musicians through the centuries have drawn on it and represented its facets in many ways. We have been left with an amazing heritage and we should use this to inspire our children. There are resource lists at the end of each of the following chapters. Try to include some of these resources on a frequent basis and encourage children to take inspiration from them.

Additional resources and experiences

- Provide an outdoor trolley or storage bay where children know they can access a range of high quality creative materials at all times – card and paper in different colours and sizes, scissors, sticky tape, clipboards and a range of fabrics, some in small pieces, some larger, with different textures and colours.

- In addition to this, you may wish to provide more specific materials to help children experiment and make choices, e.g. if children wish to draw snowdrops offer dark paper, white crayons and paint, as well as varying shades of green paint, pens or crayons.

Natural materials

Throughout this book there are ideas for collecting different materials in different seasons. Some items will last for several months and provide endless opportunities for imaginative play. They need to be stored so that children know where they are and can access them as they wish while they are playing. Large weatherproof plant pots can be used to keep them or you could use a small storage unit with clear drawers or open boxes. Natural resources commonly available through the year are shells, pebbles and stones (depending on the age of the children), fir cones, small pieces of wood and bark, small or medium logs cut into small circular sections, feathers and leaves. Seasonal items may include catkins, conkers, sycamore seeds, flower seed heads, spring blossom, autumn leaves, acorns and chestnuts.

It is important, if possible, to provide spaces where children can create patterns with natural materials, safe in the knowledge that they can come back to them to revisit and reinvent. This may be difficult in settings used by different children at different times of the day. Using a camera will at least create a photographic record for a child if the design has to be moved. Andy Goldsworthy is a contemporary British artist who works outside throughout the year using natural materials to create inspiring designs and work. Children need to experience the seasons and then they could see some of these before attempting to create something of their own. There are many images of his work to be found on the internet in a general search, including ideas for using his work to inspire young children.

Being imaginative

Imagination is developed when children are able to explore and discover for themselves. They will be inspired through play to invent and create worlds of their own, works of art, musical compositions and songs, rhymes, stories and dances.

Additional resources and experiences

ROLE-PLAY

- Outdoor space offers greater opportunities for both structured role-play and free imaginative play. A shed may be turned into a summer ice-cream shop or a spring-time garden centre. In the autumn in may be a fire station and in winter a grotto for Christmas toys.

- Children need a range of moveable materials that will allow them to build and construct using their own ideas. Offer plastic crates, ropes and pulleys, cones, marker tape, gutters and pipes of different lengths and some pieces of hosepipe. Small ladders can be used in many ways and will encourage imaginative play.

- Children need to make their own spaces and will use dens and shelters. They will build from loose parts and our job is to encourage and provide additional resources as children need them to extend and develop the play. A box of mobile phones and rucksacks may be used as they build a spaceship, whilst some large logs can be moved to create a swamp for crocodiles.

- As children explore sand and mud, they will often invent stories, make cakes or have a party for their friends. This can be developed with older children by encouraging them to draw some of the cakes or make invitations. They can invent recipes for the mud and flower cakes and take pictures of them.

- Encourage children to observe movement in the world outside through the year, and then to move in different ways. Music and art can inspire children and there are resource lists at the end of each section on seasons and elements.

CREATIVE MUSICAL EXPLORATION

- Babies will enjoy making music outside if you present objects made from different materials for them to roll, hit and shake. As children get older they may use instruments as they dance, sing and move inspired by the world around them.

- Encourage children to use instruments, rhymes and songs at all times. Join in the spontaneous singing that often occurs as children play. Introduce songs and rhymes about the world around them. Outdoor spaces offer so much more freedom. There will be times when a designated space is the main area for music-making but also times when children respond wherever they are and whatever they are doing. An outdoor music area can be used throughout the year. Supply a range of hanging instruments with beaters securely fixed nearby. Metal or wooden pipes can be cut to different lengths for children to become familiar with pitch. Fabric lengths in soft and bright colours may encourage children to move or dance as they play.

Conclusion

In addition to the actual physical resources you have provided in the environment, and also specifically for each of the curriculum areas, the most important additional resource is a responsive and sensitive adult.

Adult attitudes will shape the way children learn more than you can possibly realise. The way you pick up and hold a tiny baby, talking quietly or singing, introducing a gentle rocking rhythm is part of your natural response. This response needs to be maintained and developed as we respond to the needs of the developing baby into a lively, demanding toddler and then a curious two-year-old and an even more adventurous three-year-old. Children thrive on the relationships they have with adults and will model some of their reactions and behaviour directly in the way we react and respond.

If we are able to maintain an infectious enthusiasm and respond to the world around us in a positive and meaningful way, this will promote learning. Similarly, if we acknowledge that there is so much we need to discover and learn ourselves, and show the children some of the ways we do this, they, too, will develop a thirst for learning and knowledge.

Recommended books

Andy Goldsworthy: Collaboration with Nature by Andy Goldsworthy (Abrams 1998).
Wood by Andy Goldsworthy and Terry Friedman (Thames and Hudson 2010).
Natural: Simple Land Art Through the Seasons by Marc Pouyet (Frances Lincoln 2009). This book shows creations made with natural materials through the seasons and is designed to open a child's eyes to all the elements nature has to offer.

Nature's Playground – Activities, Crafts and Games to Encourage Children to Get Outdoors by Fiona Danks and Jo Schofield (Frances Lincoln 2006).
The Big Alfie Out of Doors Story Book by Shirley Hughes (Red Fox 1994).
RSPB Pocket Nature Wildlife of Britain (Dorling Kindersley 2009).
A First Book of Nature by Nicola Davies and Mark Kearld (Walker 2012).

4 | Working in partnership with parents

Introduction

Working in partnership with parents and carers is an essential part of good practice. Parents are the child's first and most enduring educators and have a crucial part to play in learning and development. The EYFS acknowledges that children learn to be strong and independent through positive relationships. Children are acutely aware of the relationship between their parents and their other carers, and in particular the relationship between a parent or main carer and a key worker in a setting. Children need a consistency of approach. This, however, is not always easy to achieve. Some parents may be fearful of letting children be outside and would prefer to see safety tarmac rather than a woodland floor. Similarly, they may not wish their child to be outdoors in cold or wet weather. There may be specific cultural norms and traditions which relate to the way children are expected to behave outside. Language may also be a barrier to effective communication. There are, however, many benefits to engaging families in outdoor learning. Some may not have access to outdoor spaces and if you are able to involve the whole family in your outdoor space they will be able to play and learn together. As parents become more confident about being outdoors with their children they may feel able to spend more family time outdoors at weekends. By sharing your enthusiasm you will encourage the less confident and motivate the less active families to use their local spaces and enjoy quality time with their children.

Developing your outdoor space

Any developments you make to your outdoor environment and curriculum need to be shared with parents. If you are planning major changes to your outdoor space, parents may be able to help in many ways and it is useful to do a skills audit and involve as many parents as possible. Most parents are always concerned about how and what their children are learning and a few may not necessarily see playing outside as an intrinsic part of the learning process. It is vitally important that you are able to explain the nature of play and help parents understand the ways in which children can learn outdoors. As you develop outdoor learning opportunities for the children, use photographs and displays that explain the benefits for children. Explain why children need to be outside every day and how you can work together to make sure children are suitably dressed for the weather and the season. If you have a reasonably large space, consider creating areas where parents can sit together with their families or with each other. Just being outside together will help them to relax and begin to enjoy the special nature of the outdoors.

Venturing further afield

If you are able to encourage parents to get outside with their children particularly at weekends on in holiday periods, this can have an important effect on the way children respond when with you and vice versa. Open up discussion on how and why parents should take children outside and begin to share the joys of the natural world with them.

When you have been out for a walk with children, think about making a map and sending it home so that parents can take children on the same walk if they wish. Children will love to take a lead role in the family outing, as they relate to their parents what they observed and discussed when out with you.

Make a display in your entrance hall showing pictures of local places to visit, or design a leaflet with suggestions of places to go with children that are accessible by public transport as well as by car. Encourage parents to tell you where they have been with their children, to bring in photographs of time spent outside and maybe bring in anything they find which can be used in the children's play.

During school holiday periods many organisations are now offering a range of outdoor activities. Try to research these in advance and talk to parents about them. Some will be free and others may make a charge. Rock pooling with experts and a poetry workshop about sea creatures were just two free events we found last summer. Research your local wildlife trusts for holiday activities. National Trust venues offer many different events for children of different age groups. There is usually an admission charge to the properties unless the family has annual membership, although we have discovered a wonderful natural play trail which is open to all and just involves a car park fee or a bus ride. One local council imports sand and creates a large beach near the river during the school summer holiday.

Special events

Some settings are now holding outdoor workshops for parents and there is particular emphasis on the role of fathers and male carers. There may be a specific focus for events according to the time of year. Planting vegetables in the spring, a summer picnic, autumn bonfire and winter barbecue could be arranged. All activities need to be carefully planned and if they are popular there may need to be a booking system.

A recent project in Oxfordshire (Without Walls) describes how a family worker was able to make home visits to Asian families and explain why it is important to get children outside. They stress the importance of getting to know parents and what they actually think about being outdoors. For many it is unfamiliar and they may be fearful of the cold or getting messy. Talking to parents is an important first step in encouraging them to be outside with their children. The staff then arranged family visits to local places of interest so parents could attend with their children.

One practitioner in a children's centre started to take out groups of children under three with their parents to a local park. She structured the sessions around forest school principles but adapted them to take the young age of the children into account. When she moved away from the setting the parents were so enthusiastic they decided to continue to run the group themselves. One of them was willing to act as a leader and she is now interested in training to be a forest school practitioner. In the meantime, she plans a focus for each of the weekly sessions. Parents contribute a small amount of money, which is used to buy snacks, water and any materials needed such as string, scissors and a first aid kit. They have decided to name the group Treetots.

Case study

Treetots

It was a damp drizzly morning but this did not deter the Treetots. The leader arrived early, laid a groundsheet and erected a tarpaulin roof tied from the trees. While she went off to lay a trail other parents arrived and the children explored the immediate woodland space. Today there were nine children and seven parents. The ages of the children ranged from twelve months to three years. Some of them knew each other but two were new to the group.

Initial exploration included looking very closely at a rotten tree stump and discussions about the creatures they found. Parents encouraged children to observe but to treat the creatures with respect and replace any pieces of wood they moved. One tree stump was hollow and there was discussion about what could live inside.

H: I think it's a bear.

M: No ten bears!

Adult: I wonder what the bears like to eat.

H: Me!

Several large holes were also a focal point as adults talked to children about what might live there. Children used sticks to poke in the soil and mud. They were all very involved in their immediate environment. Parents explained how an old tree had fallen to the ground but pointed out that new trees were forming from the old branches. Another one talked about old leaves going mushy and making soft spongy soil. One path led under some very low branches and children held them up for each other to get underneath. There was long wet grass and a variety of flowering grasses and plants.

After around half an hour the children came together to sit on the groundsheet and new people were introduced as everyone said their names. The children were shown some laminated leaf shapes in yellow and green as these were the markers for the trail. Along the trail were different challenges. Printed instructions had been set out for parents to read to their child and encourage them to engage in discussion or an activity. They had to look closely at a hole under a tree and decide what animal might live there – a cow, a rabbit, an elephant or a fox.

One parent spotted a baby robin on a branch and children watched quietly as the parent bird hopped on the floor nearby looking for food.

Another challenge was to use some logs and sticks from a pile to make a small xylophone. The two new children were fascinated by this and spent several minutes tapping different lengths of sticks and logs. The youngest twelve-month-old enjoyed crawling on the ground and feeling different textures.

The next challenge along the trail was to collect fallen leaves of different shapes and match them to the laminated shapes. A big tree stump made an ideal table to lay out the leaves and look more closely at them. The trail led to a large oak tree. A notice was attached to the tree: 'Can you hold hands with everyone and see if we can make a circle round this tree?' This led to the children and adults singing. Words were improvised as they sang to the tune of 'Here we go round the Mulberry bush': 'Here we go round a very big tree, a very big tree, a very big tree / On a cold and rainy morning.'

The trail concluded with a hunt for a treasure box. Two crossed sticks and a laminated sign made the X sign. 'X marks the spot' said two children. The box contained cereal bars and was carefully carried back to the den space. The children ate them together with raisins and fresh water. As they sat they were able to listen to rain on the tarpaulin roof and a robin singing in a nearby tree. At the end of the session while the adults took down the tarpaulin three children went back along the path. They looked down the hollow tree trunk:

'We need to find that bear.'
'He's asleep.'
'Shall we wake him?'
'Yes, but he might be hungry.'
'He needs his breakfast. I can smell hot dogs.'

Everyone agreed that despite the damp and the rain they had all enjoyed themselves. On the way back three children found a very muddy puddle and the parents allowed them to spend some time stamping around in it together. Parents and children worked together at the end to find ways of cleaning up the wellies!

This observation shows how very young children and their parents can benefit from spending time together in a group. A brief analysis of the observation also shows that learning occurs across the Foundation Stage curriculum and children are moving towards many of the early learning goals. The three prime curriculum areas were at the forefront of the session.

Personal, social and emotional development

Making relationships

Although there was a wide age range in this group children seemed to be very aware of each other and responded appropriately to the needs of any individual child. The older ones held up the tree branches for the little ones and it was interesting to observe how new children quickly became part of the group. The new child, who was two, began to share with another two-year-old in the group. They held out dandelion heads to each other before speaking but by the end of the session were moving round together.

Self-confidence and self-awareness

Children who had attended the sessions on a regular basis were confident in the outdoor environment. Initially, the two newer children appeared less confident, moved less freely and needed more adult support. However as they developed an awareness of the dynamics of the session and the freedom they were given to explore and discover things, to spend time looking at something of their choice, they became more confident. Children in this group have the added confidence that is given by having a parent or carer around. Parents seemed to operate on a shared basis, initiating and joining in conversations with other children in the group.

Managing feelings and behaviour

Children were aware of the physical boundaries and the rules of the group. Parents talked to them about treating the environment with respect, e.g. replacing pieces of wood and not disturbing the habitats of some of the creatures they discovered. At a very young age they were learning to respect other group members and also the world around them. Children worked very much as a group despite their young ages. They helped children who were not always so confident or needed extra help.

Physical development

Moving and handling

The uneven ground presented challenges for the younger children and also the new children. Older children moved confidently and safely up and down small hills, over tree stumps and roots and through long, wet grass. Younger children watched them and were able to follow, sometimes with help from an adult. Fallen trees gave children the chance to climb and use their whole bodies.

One two-year-old wanted to climb up on a tree trunk. It was a bit slippery but after the third attempt she managed it and stood on the top clapping her hands.

Fine motor movements were encouraged as the children picked up tiny leaves or seeds from the ground. They used sticks of different lengths, sometimes as walking sticks or musical instruments or just something to carry.

Moving in a group was encouraged as they made the circle around the tree. It took some time for all children to understand the idea and to join in. Then they were able to move round in a circle because there was a high adult-child ratio.

Health and self-care

Children came well dressed for a rainy session. Parents were now experienced in the use of appropriate clothing and these children will grow up with the concept that they can go out in all weathers and have a really good time. One parent from Canada said, 'Now we've come to live here I figured they have to get used to rain!'

The children all became deeply involved in the immediate space and this in itself led to a state of well-being and emotional balance. They were able to use a large space to exercise and at times some of the older ones just ran around in large circles in the green spaces as well as enjoying the woodland paths.

A large tarpaulin sheltered the Treetots as they ate their snack and listened to the robin and the raindrops on the roof.

Healthy food was offered at snack time and all children were thrilled to receive a cereal bar, a drink of water and some raisins.

Communication and language

Parents used their first languages and English as they spoke to their children. In this small group other languages used were French, Dutch, Chinese and Hungarian. Parents were encouraged to talk to their own children and to others in the group. There was a high level of verbal interaction. Children talked to their parents and as they became more confident, they talked to each other about what they could see, hear and touch.

Listening and attention

Children responded to the language used by their parents as well as English. They were also able to sit in a group. They listened intently to the sound of the rain and the singing of the robin.

Understanding

Younger children were able to understand the idea of following the trail as they had visual clues as well as being able to watch older children. As they joined in the different challenges, adults used language that was appropriate for the children to follow the instructions.

Speaking

Children talked about their experiences all the time. There was discussion about real creatures as well as imaginary ones.

Additional curriculum areas of learning

Mathematics: Shape, space and measure

Children used sticks of different lengths and laid them out in order of length. They matched leaf shapes to laminated templates. As sticks were laid in a row two children spontaneously began to count them.

Understanding the world: People and communities

Children heard a variety of languages being spoken by other parents to their children.

Understanding the world: The world

The children looked at the roots of trees and heard about the way the roots are needed for growth. They observed at first hand a range of small minibeasts in their home habitats. They talked about different colours of leaves, and watched a robin caring for its young chick. They listened to a detailed explanation of the way decaying material forms new soil and nutrients on the ground.

Expressive arts and design: Exploring and using media and materials

Children used pieces of wood to make different sounds by banging and tapping. They joined in singing, both in a group around the tree and also as individuals when sharing the tapping experience with their parents.

Expressive arts and design: Being imaginative

The conversations of the three-year-olds showed highly developed imaginations. They invented bears and other creatures that lived in the woods. There was discussion, too, about who might live down the holes on the bank.

In addition to offering a vital learning experience for the children, the group offered many benefits for the parents. They were all enthusiastic about the experience and admitted that on their own they would not normally go out with their child in the rain. The group offered emotional support to parents from different cultures, and by providing questions and challenges, parents were encouraged to talk to their children and to each other. Parents seemed to get just as involved with looking down holes, finding creatures and following the trail as their children. Children with additional needs were treated with respect and understanding, and again parents felt that they were part of a group.

Parents' perspective on the Treetots under-fives group (with thanks to Sue)

This was a written response to the questions in an informal questionnaire.

How long have you been coming to this group?
Six weeks.

Do you mind going out in wet or cold weather?
Usually I moan about it, but I love everything about getting the kids outdoors, though. Also, I struggle a bit with depression in the dark winters here, so am hoping this will break that vicious winter cycle of not finding the enthusiasm to get us outside.

What have you enjoyed about the sessions?
I completely love the setting – the trees, the greenness of it all, the lack of cultivation, of feeling like a gardener's just been through. Easier to breathe out there, you know? And I love to see my kids free to wander, alone or with others, to explore both the setting – the bugs, the soil, the twigs, etc, and what they can do in it – build, break, collect, sort, etc. And both of those aspects on much grander scales, too – the size of the trees, the fields, the sky, and their running and climbing and dragging and throwing.

Also, the other mums and the kids. Always, a precious space where you can connect with other mums, laugh and talk and share. And sigh. Vent frustrations, look for new ideas, be inspired or just reminded that you're not the only one. I guess in terms of this group, I feel a bit less out of place than I do with most other groups of mums, because of the setting and that they've chosen to be in this one. Is it silly to say it kind of feels like it's on my territory, because it's a forest? I am more relaxed about being me.

And I love that I can let them wander out of my sight. No one is watching my parenting. I can relax a little – not constantly feeling like some other adult needs to hear me scolding or directing them.

And I guess, I feel like it's letting me share with my kids a little bit more of me – of what I care about apart from the house and family. (Daddy's side of the family don't really like the outdoors – there's no telly!) I want them to know the wilderness, the peace of just being outside, and this park is as close as we can get at the moment, and it's great.

What do you think are the benefits for the children?
The fresh air, the outdoors, the exercise. My children are growing up British – they better learn to cope with the rain!

The friendships, and the learning to be with a group – doing what is required at times, sitting on the tarpaulin, singing the hello song, sharing a snack. But also the freedom to wander and explore, to participate in the activity or not, or to modify it as they see fit.

The weekly routine.

Mummy being happy. (That is a big one!)

The self-awareness and confidence that comes from having a go at things – climbing a big log, jumping a mud-puddle. For the little one, just walking through slippery mud in welly boots, or copying what the big kids do – collecting sticks, etc. Falling on her face and recovering – it's important, I think.

Being outside in a group together provides quality time for both parents and their children.

Having things to tell Daddy about when he gets home at night.

Extending their imaginative play, both by sharing games and story lines with friends and adults, and by finding new settings or objects that prompt new ideas or directions.

Knowing that he (almost four) is trusted to be sensible – if he goes off he can find his way back, and will come back soon, or if he is called. And that he will take care of smaller kids.

He's not interested in arts and crafts activities, but that's fine too – he knows he doesn't have to do them, but that some of the other kids like to. They are all recognised as individuals, perhaps mostly because we mums are there, but there's no feeling of being pressured to fit in, be and do the same as everyone else, be part of your class, or whatever. And for her, the crafty activities, because we don't do much of that at home yet.

And of course I'm hoping there will be longer-term benefits, that they may become adults who can entertain themselves outside, even (gasp!) choose to be outside sometimes!

What does your child enjoy about it?
Exploring, climbing, and seeing his favourite girlfriend. He does get involved in the nitty-gritty of looking closely at bugs and things, but is more into running through the trees.

And talking – telling stories with the adults, telling the kids what to do!

She (18 months) just loves being able to follow big kids around, and try and copy them. Happy toddler!

Do you think it has helped your child in any way?
We sleep well on Friday nights! And it's given him lots of new things to ask three-year-old questions about – wish I'd written them down!

Seriously, I do think it's great for both of them, for all of us.

Conclusion

Mummy being happy! This seems to sum up the nature of partnership. A parent who is happy and relaxed will have the confidence and patience that is needed for the toughest job in the world. Parents who can spend quality time outdoors with their children will enable their children to make the most of the additional opportunities offered by an early years setting. Invite your families to take part in festivals and special events outdoors. Parents will often volunteer to help with taking children outside on walks and visits. If they are involved in the planning, they will also understand the potential for learning and be able to encourage and inspire children. This was evident in the case study where parents modelled the good practice of the practitioner and were able to sustain the group, with the concurring benefits for both themselves and their young children. They were particularly interested to read the case study observations and the way in which they showed progress in the areas of learning. Two of them are now keen to undergo further training.

Reference sources

National Trust: www.nationaltrust.org.uk
National wildlife trusts: www.wildlifetrusts.org
www.growingschools.org.uk
Search for places to visit near you.

www.netmums.com
Lists activities and events in your local area.

www.walkswithbuggies.com
Excellent website covering all regions, with many suggestions of walks suitable for pushchairs and young children.

Without Walls – Creative Work with Families Developing the Outdoor Space – A Resource for Children's Centre's Managers and Staff, compiled by Julia Sargent (2009), Oxfordshire County Council.
Obtainable from earlyyearspublications@oxfordshire.gov.uk or Learning through Landscapes, email: enquiries@ltl.org.uk.

Advice sheet: *Playnotes: Families Outdoors* (July 2010).
Available from Learning through Landscapes at www.ltl.org.uk.

Part 2 | The four seasons

When asked to choose their favourite season, many adults find it difficult to name just one. Immediately a host of images and memories flood into the mind. Often our decision is based on our childhood experiences, and even as adults many of our favourite seasonal pastimes are a continuation of the experiences of our youth. We may still find great pleasure in scrunching through autumn leaves or splashing through puddles. We may dash outside at the first sign of snow and build a snowman or hunt for a sledge. In summer we love to go the sea, lie on the sand and splash in waves. We have favourite recollections of each season and conversely, there are probably things we dislike about each season. Summer can bring on intense heat or drought, a plague of wasps, but also the glory of a meadow in bloom and apples ripening on trees. Winter is dark and cold but that also means cosy evenings, maybe lighting a fire or a brisk walk on a sunny day when the ground is layered with frost. Whatever our joys or dislikes, the fact remains, that our lives are governed by this rhythmic cycle through each year. Spring brings hope after winter and many of us look forward to a new year with optimism. Let us use each new year to make the most of every day. Take children outside and explore with them the changing and dynamic world in which we live. We are truly fortunate to have such a richness and depth of sensory experiences in each of our four seasons.

The following four chapters pick out the most common features of each time of year. Children will make their own discoveries and there are useful sources of reference which may help them to identify things and answer some of their questions. There are suggestions for conversations and stories to reinforce and extend the first-hand experience. Exploring the seasons with young children is a time of discovery and learning for everyone. We need to enter into the world of the child and see the world around us through their eyes. As companion learners, we will offer them something special which they can build into their own experiences and which will stay with them through adult life.

5 | Spring

Introduction

The official first day of spring is around the 21st March, as this is the point in space and time when the sun moves across the celestial equator from south to north. Weather conditions are generally more unstable and there will be days during late February and early March that seem to be warmer and herald the onset of spring. Conversely, there may be days after 21 March when it is frosty and cold, and often there is snow in some areas of the country. Climate change and global warming seem to be adding to this confusion and there are reported sightings of some insects and plants very early in the year, which then disappear again with the onset of late frosts and snow. One of the most noticeable factors is the increase in daylight hours and children will be able to observe this. It is caused by the axis of the earth increasing its tilt toward the sun, so that with the increased light there is an increase in warmth, which in turn increases new growth. Flowers and trees are showing signs of colour and buds are swelling. Birdsong is more prominent and in rural settings it may be possible to observe baby lambs and calves.

This chapter encourage us to be aware of new life and growth all around us in the natural world. There is a focus on planting flowers and vegetables and also the wildlife beginning to emerge in the garden and surrounding countryside.

Walks in spring

Try to take children out in small groups if possible. If you have a local park or even some woodland space, children will enjoy looking out for different signs of spring, new leaves and blossom on the trees, or spring bulbs in the flowerbeds. Even walking along a pavement will be different, as there may be gardens to look at, plants and trees and even dandelions and daisies peeping through cracks in the concrete. When out with children try to make time to stand still and listen to the sounds around you. You may hear birds singing, and if you are in woodland, rustles from squirrels and birds in the trees. You may hear the breeze in the leaves or the sound of falling rain. Look at the different types of bark and encourage children to touch and talk about the different textures.

In the garden

Spring is the best time to plant seeds for flower and vegetable crops, although some seedlings may need to be kept indoors until the danger of frost has passed, usually around the middle of May. Even very young children can help with the planting. Older children will need less adult supervision. Plant pots can be made from newspaper or you can recycle plastic trays and yogurt pots. Make drainage holes in the bottom before you fill them with seed compost. A comprehensive guide to planting with children can be found in *Every Nursery Needs a Garden* (Watts 2011).

Planting flowers and herbs

Most flowers that are planted from seed in the spring are known as annuals as they flower and die in the same year. Sunflowers are one of the most popular to plant. *Verbena bonariensis* is good for insects and may grow taller than the children. Packets of wild flower seeds are easy to obtain, and in late spring this seed can be scattered on any spare patch of soil to create a haven for insects and pollinators.

Lavenders can be grown from seed, but it is much easier to buy small plants and let the children plant them out in baskets, containers or flowerbeds. They will grow quickly enough to flower in the same year but will last several years and provide a good source of nectar for wildlife. Most garden centres will also supply a range of herbs in small pots that children can plant out. These, too, can be grown in containers in a smaller space.

Planting potatoes

These can be planted from February onwards and there are several different varieties to choose from. They can be planted in patio containers if you have a small space or maybe in a raised vegetable bed. Jute bags make good containers and, as they have handles, this helps if you need to move the potatoes for any reason, maybe if you have a shared space. The potatoes will flourish in jute containers and children will easily be able to tip the bag over and search for the crop. If your setting is closed during August, try to plant an early crop – 'Pentland Javelin', 'Rocket' or 'Charlotte' are suitable.

Look out for:

- Varieties that are suitable for your space, either in a container or a bed, and that have an appropriate growing period.
- Eyes beginning to form on tubers.
- Small white roots that may be showing.

Talk about:

- The shapes and sizes of the tubers.
- The small eyes beginning to grow – how big will they get?
- Roots, and how they are essential to absorb moisture from the ground to keep the plant alive.
- How much space to leave between each tuber (follow the instructions on the packet or make up laminated cards for children to use); use a tape measure or stick when planting.

Supply:

- A packet of seed potatoes.
- Tools to dig over the ground and make holes.
- A suitable container or outside space.
- Water supply and watering cans.
- Pictures of various stages of growth and also harvesting, so children begin to understand the process.

Planting other vegetables

There are many types of food crops suitable for planting with young children and you may need to think of ways to include some in containers if you have a very small space. Tomatoes will grow well in a growbag and there are now some that can be grown in hanging baskets or flower pots. When planting tomato seeds, remember that each one makes a large plant so you won't need very many. They should grow fairly quickly and will need to be planted in larger pots or into the ground once there is no danger of frost, usually towards the middle of May.

Strawberries are a popular crop and can also be grown in hanging baskets or patio containers if space is limited. Pumpkins are easy to grow if you have enough space. Some vegetables from different cultures can be grown but may need a little more attention. Mizuna and mibuna are easy to grow in containers or beds. Plant Mooli radishes in May and they should be ready in about eight weeks' time.

If you have space for a raised bed in a permanent outdoor space, try planting some early peas and beans. Children can help to prepare the soil by digging it and then adding some compost. They then need to rake the soil and make a narrow trench for the seeds. Seeds can be planted in straight lines or in blocks. Each line should be marked with a named marker and maybe a laminated picture of the crop. Follow the instructions on the seed packet and help children to measure the spaces between seeds.

Look out for:

- Seed mixes suitable for children.
- Something different – one nursery has just planted loofah seeds with their youngest children to grow loofahs for the treasure baskets.
- Patio collections containing varieties of vegetables to grow in small spaces.

Talk about:

- Different shapes and sizes of seeds – carrot seeds are tiny and children need only a pinch of seed at a time; lettuce seeds, too, need to be planted thinly; tomato seeds are easier to handle and can be planted four to a flower pot and then transplanted as they get bigger.
- Why we plant in the spring, and the time it takes for crops to grow.
- Suitable growing conditions for plants – try planting some bean seeds in a pot in a dark place, some in a dry place, a cold place and a warm spot with good light; let children observe and discuss.
- The need for regular watering and weeding if you have a larger plot.
- The names of garden tools – trowel, fork, rake and hoe, and the need to use these safely; talk about looking after the tools and how to store them.

Supply:

- Peat-free compost or good soil.
- Coir compost – children enjoy adding water to this and creating their own mix.
- Seeds and photographs of plants at later stages of growth.
- Appropriate tools for children to use – most garden centres now sell attractive sets for children and children need to learn about safe handling and storage.
- Clear containers to plant beans in so children can see root growth.
- Camera to record stages of growth if you want to make a pictorial record.

Wildlife

If you have created a wildlife area in your setting, encourage children to visit it on warmer days and take time to observe any changes. There may be some flowers appearing depending on your planting. Primroses and dead nettle flower in spring and will attract early bees.

Small insects may be emerging. There may be the occasional bee or butterfly on a warm day and if you have a pond you may see frogs coming out of hibernation. Frog and toad spawn is usually laid at the end of March or during April, but this can vary according to weather conditions. Toad spawn is laid in long strips and frogspawn in large clumps.

Look out for:

- Frogs and frogspawn – if you have a small pond with a safety mesh over it children can observe first-hand the development of frogspawn and the growth of tadpoles.
- Toads, which may be sheltering under flowerpots or logs.
- Caterpillars and early butterflies, ladybirds and other small creatures.
- Butterfly eggs laid on the back of a leaf.

Talk about:

- The lifecycle of the frog, and encourage children to chat about the tadpoles and what they need to survive. How do the tadpoles swim? How do they breathe at different stages of development? What do they eat?

- Caterpillars – what do they eat? Consider the different markings on different species. Look at the patterns on them and how they move. Discuss how they will change into a chrysalis before emerging as a butterfly. Metamorphosis is a word which children will love to repeat.

- Different sounds – maybe the buzzing of an early insect, or the types of birdsong.

- Ladybirds – these make their first appearance in the spring after overwintering in a dormant state. Males and females emerge looking for early aphids to eat. They mate in the spring and the female lays eggs in late spring. This generation of adults then dies as the new generation hatches out in the summer. There are 27 species commonly recognised in the UK but the most common is the seven-spot red ladybird.

Supply:

- Reference books with pictures to help children identify wildlife (see list at end of chapter) and learn about life cycles.

- Magnifying glasses lenses and pooters for close observation.

- Suitable plant pots, stones and pieces of wood for children to make a 'bug palace' – a habitat to encourage small insects, which can be built on a base and include lengths of canes, old flowerpots on their sides and air bricks.

- A pile of old logs and rotting wood to attract small creatures.

- Plastic wildlife creatures for children to use in their play – maybe in the sand or on a rockery.

New growth

Flowers

By the beginning of March, the snowdrops will be disappearing but suddenly outdoor spaces are full of colour as daffodils, crocus and tulips emerge. Primroses can be found in the wild, but it is now possible to buy plants in garden centres and use them in your own space. Daffodils and narcissus are in full bloom and during April it is possible to see tulips in many different colours. If you have not planted any in your setting, it may be worth taking a walk to a local park to look at its flower displays. Encourage younger children to look at the colours of plants and flowers and if children are able to pick any flowers from your own garden, they may be able to use them as a centrepiece at a meal or snack table.

Look out for:

- Different varieties of spring bulbs – blue Muscari (grape hyacinth); small crocus in shades of yellow, white and purple; daffodils and narcissus; tulips in bright colours.
- Flowers that children can view closely – encourage children to look carefully inside the petals to see the stamens and pollen sacs.

Talk about:

- Different shades of yellow, the way daffodils move in the breeze, the pale yellow of primroses and the crinkly texture of their leaves.
- The deep colours of tulips.
- How the stems and flowers have emerged from the bulbs that children planted in the autumn – use photographs to remind them of this.
- The need to encourage insects and wildlife by planting these flowers.

Supply:

- Clipboards outside and good quality art materials in a range of shades (children in a Reggio Emilia preschool were able to choose from at least ten shades of yellow crayons when drawing spring flowers).
- Lenses and magnifiers for children to look closely at the structure of the flowerhead.

Wild flowers

Even if you have a limited outdoor area it is usually possible to discover daisies and dandelions pushing their heads through cracks in walls and pavements. Children need to learn that some wild flowers, particularly those growing in the countryside, should not be picked, but it is usually possible to pick dandelions and daisies growing in a lawn, hedge or wall. Blowing dandelion clocks is a time-honoured tradition and children can be encouraged to look at the formation of the seed heads and parachutes.

Similarly, children might enjoy making daisy chains, although this is difficult for very young children and they may need adult help.

Buttercups, too, push through in early spring and children love to pick them and hold them under each other's chins to see if there is a yellow reflection. Traditionally this is supposed to show whether the friend likes butter or not.

Bluebells are a familiar sight to some in the spring time, but bluebell woods are not always accessible to many. Some parks have a wild space where bluebells seem to thrive, so it is worth trying to find out if there are any near enough for you to take children out.

Shrubs and trees

Many shrubs and small trees are particularly attractive at this time of year and can be included in your planting layout if you have your own outdoor space. Otherwise you may be able to take the children to a nearby park or garden to look at the blossom, flowers and new leaves which come out during late March, April and May. Our local school includes a neighbour's front garden on its spring walk, as there is a beautiful magnolia tree in flower. I can remember, as a child, lying under a cherry tree and staring up at a brilliant blue sky. It brings to mind the words of A. E. Housman:

Loveliest of trees, the cherry now is hung with bloom along the bough

Fruit trees carry blossom and as the petals fall in late spring, tiny fruits begin to form.

Look out for:

- New buds unfurling – the sticky buds of a horse chestnut tree are always appealing.
- Delicate new leaves of different colours on acer trees.
- Catkins on willow and hazel trees.
- Pussy willow on willow trees.
- Flower spikes on chestnut trees in late spring.
- Cherry blossom in different shades of pink and white; if children can collect this they can use it in their play – they will enjoy using it in a variety of ways, maybe as play food, in 'potions' or to create patterns or pictures with paint or glue.
- Fruit trees that are in blossom and then showing tiny fruits after pollination.

Talk about:

- The need for warmth, light and moisture for new buds to develop.
- The shapes and textures of the unfurling chestnut buds.
- Different shades of green as buds begin to open on shrubs and trees – consider the contrast in the shades of green as you look at a budding larch tree (a deciduous conifer); compare it with a dark evergreen conifer.
- The Japanese custom 'Hanami', which celebrates the viewing of the cherry blossom (sakura). It is said to be a symbolic representation of clouds. Japanese families celebrate by picnicking under the cherry trees; if you have a tree nearby maybe you could do the same.
- The role of bees and insects in pollinating flowers and fruits.

Supply:

- Clipboards, paper and coloured pastels.
- A camera for children to record buds at different stages of development.
- A range of art materials outdoors for children to use to draw blossom and leaves.
- Containers for them to collect blossom.
- Small pots and water so they can add blossom and petals to make 'perfume'.
- Spaces for creative designs using natural materials.

Case study

Spring

One nursery school has a treehouse built into a cherry tree. Children are very aware of the blossom, and this shows in their conversations.

L: Do you want to hear the good news?
Adult: Ooh, yes please.
L: Its blossom everywhere – there's blossom even on the soil.
Some while later he said: The problem is – it's all going to fall and die.
Children looking at the blossom on the ground:
  — Its soft, it's ticklish.
  — Its pink – it looks like our own bed.
Children lay down in the blossom
T. in the tree: I like being up with the blossom.
K: Let's play a game with blossom – I'll count and you can throw blossom on this pile.

The next day the children used small brushes to sweep the blossom into piles. They filled containers and carried them to a table where they had a blossom kitchen. Using a variety of kitchen utensils they created imaginary pies, cakes and pancakes. Some children were investigating the blossom by touching, looking at it closely, patting it and describing the texture: 'soft, pink, wet'.

Adult: Let me give you some of this. What does it taste like?
Child: (pretending to eat it) It's not nice.
Adult: Is it too sour? Shall we add some sugar?

More petals were added and the children agreed it tasted better. As they played, they joined in a song led by the adult.

> Pop a little pancake into the pan (x 3)
> That's for my dinner today,
> Shake on the sugar with a shake, shake, shake (x 3)
> That's for my dinner today
> Squeeze on the lemon with a squeeze, squeeze, squeeze (x 3)
> That's for my dinner today
> Roll it up with a roly poly poly (x 3)
> That's for my dinner today

Pop it in your mouth with a yum, yum, yum (x 3)
That's for my dinner today.

Adult comment:

This song happened when I asked one of the children pretending to cook with a frying pan, 'What are you cooking?' and she replied 'Pancake'. Other children playing alongside joined in with the singing. Did you notice that as the singing got louder more children joined the group and asked 'What are you doing?'

Here the adult was able to encourage children to play imaginatively, but also linked in a song with repetitive, easy-to-learn phrases so children who were learning English found it easy to join in.

Children spent many days playing with the blossom, either where it had fallen on the ground or carrying it to other places. They lay in it, swept it up, threw it, collected it and mixed it up with other elements. Some children wanted to climb higher to touch it and moved climbing apparatus to enable this. They also put soft toys up into the tree. Appropriate art materials encouraged children to paint pictures of blossom.

Baby animals

Children who live in the countryside will be very aware of the arrival of new lambs and calves. City children, too, may be able to visit a farm for first-hand experience, or watch a DVD about a farm in spring. Baby chicks and ducklings can be seen and now some settings are able to raise their own. Some farms offer an incubator scheme where they supply the equipment and fertile eggs together with instructions on care. You may, however, need to find suitable homes for the new babies. Children are fascinated as they watch the hatching process and learn how to care for the chicks or ducklings.

Look out for:

- Neighbourhood farms that allow visits from groups of young children.
- Suitable DVDs or TV programmes showing new animals.
- Animals in surrounding fields if you are in a rural setting.

Learning about new growth is important as these children care for their young chicks.

Talk about:

- Why farm animals are born in the spring – more grass for them to eat; longer time of warmth before the next winter.
- How they are cared for by their mothers.
- Textures – fluffy chicks; woolly lambs (link this to sheep shearing in summer and talk about items made from wool).
- How many days it will be until the eggs hatch out and how to care for baby chicks – what do they need?

Supply:

- Pictures, photographs and video clips of newborn lambs and chicks.
- Suitable art materials to enable children to create pictures of animals.
- Picture books and stories.
- An incubator with eggs.

Counting the days until the eggs hatch develops an understanding of number and progression of time. Clear photographs help all children to understand the process.

Birds in the spring

This is a good time for children to observe birds as they become very active and can be more easily seen in the bushes and trees that haven't yet grown their leaves. Birds are beginning to pair up and children may observe the differences between male and female in several species. Birds still benefit from extra food supplies so continue to feed them, particularly in colder spells. Try putting out some pieces of wool, soft fluff or moss and see if the birds collect it for nest materials. Nest boxes should have been cleaned during winter months and birds will be showing an interest. Nest box cameras are now readily available and if you are able to set one up this will give children a rare insight into the laying of eggs, incubation and the hatching of baby chicks. Encourage children to stand still and listen to birdsong on a sunny spring day.

Look out for:

- Birds pairing up and displaying to each other.
- Birds carrying nesting materials in their beaks and building nests.
- The arrival of swallows in late April as they fly back from Africa.

Talk about:

- How birdsong is different in spring from the bird sounds we get later in the year. There are long sequences of sound and this is bound up with the need to find a mate. Usually it is the male that is singing; the sound is rich and uplifting.
- The different sizes and shape of nests, according to the species. If you have an old nest from last year, let children examine it and see how the birds have woven the materials together. Discuss where they might have found all the materials.
- How we can help the birds by continuing to feed them.

Supply:

- Reference books or identification charts of bird species.
- Nest boxes – these should be put up early in the year.
- A nest box camera and viewing screen, if you have the funding and suitable space.
- Small binoculars for children to use.
- Small twigs, moss, feathers and lichen for children to experiment with nest-building.
- Bird food for children to keep feeders topped up.

Spring celebrations

Easter is the main festival we celebrate during this season. The name 'Easter' derives from a pagan Saxon goddess called 'Eastre'. The first Sunday after the full moon was named Easter Day, and Eastre's symbols were the hare and the egg. As hares are not so common, this symbol has been replaced by the rabbit and so we have the tradition of the Easter Bunny as well as Easter eggs. The name is still used but celebrates new life. Christians celebrate the resurrection of Jesus.

Another festival held in spring is the first day of May. Traditionally Morris dancers greet the morning. Maypole dancing takes place in many towns and villages and is popular, and some villages may crown a 'May Queen'. This is something that families can enjoy watching together.

Conclusion

As spring moves on into summer, you may need to look at ideas in the next chapter. Our changing weather patterns often mean that spring in the natural world seems to arrive earlier. Flowers bloom earlier and birds begin nest-building. However, sometimes the weather can change and a late snowfall can have disastrous consequences. We need to help children to be aware of this and do all they can to help plants and bird life to survive in cold weather. Conversely, there may be very hot days in April and May which equate to summer, and again this will affect the world around us. Children and adults should enjoy the surge of spring growth and feel the natural energy around them.

Further resources

Spring stories

A Seed in Need by Sam Godwin (Wayland 1998).
Ferdie's Springtime Blossom by Julia Rawlinson (Gullane Children's Books 2010).
Jasper's Beanstalk by Nick Butterworth (Hodder Children's Books 2008).
The Listening Walk by Paul Showers (Harper Collins 1993).
The Tiny Seed by Eric Carle (Puffin 1997).

Small world play

Life cycle stages: The Frog: The Ladybug: The Butterfly: The Ant. Plastic models of creatures at all stages from Insect Lore from www.amazon.co.uk.

Reference books and websites

All Year Round: A Calendar of Celebrations (Festivals and the Seasons) by C. Fynes Clinton, M. Rowling and A. Druitt (Hawthorn Press 1995).
How Do Plants Grow? (Young Explorer World of Plants) by Louise and Richard Spilsbury (Heinemann 2006).
How a Seed Grows – Let's Read and Find Out Science by Helene Jordan (Harper Collins 2000).
www.think-differently-about-sheep.com
www.bbc.co.uk/berkshire/content/articles/2008/04/10/dawn_chorus_birdsong_feature. shtml
www.ladybird-survey.org

Spring music

'Spring' from *The Four Seasons* by Vivaldi.
Rite of Spring by Igor Stravinsky.
Morning has Broken recorded by Cat Stevens (1972).

Spring art

Pictures by David Hockney: *Woldgate Lane to Burton Agnes* (2008); *Three trees near Thixendale Spring* (2008); *Early blossom Woldgate* (2009).
These can either be bought as posters or displayed via a projector onto a screen for children to talk about and work on their own interpretation of spring flowers and blossom. See www.hockneypictures.com.

Other prints obtainable from www.art.co.uk:
Spring Flowers by Annie Feray Mutrie (good illustration of primroses) (1856).
Peach Tree in Bloom by Vincent van Gogh (1888).
Verger avec pruniers en Fleurs by Vincent van Gogh (1888).
Blossoming Chestnut Branches by Vincent van Gogh (c. 1890).
Pear Tree by Vincent van Gogh (1888).
Trees and Flowers, Spring at Pontoise by Camille Pissarro (1877).
Le Printemps by Claude Monet (1900).

6 | Summer

Introduction

Summer is a season that conjures up visions of 'lazy hazy' days but which in reality can be the most unreliable of all our seasons in that it does not always live up to our expectations. Very often there are long periods of wet or cold weather or sunny days may be hotter than we would like.

Children are happy outdoors at all times of the year, but it is often the case that adults need much less persuasion to be outside when the sun is shining. There is a feel-good factor that is important for our health and well-being. Children will be able to create their own play scenarios and hopefully have long periods of uninterrupted outdoor play, which will enable them, too, to relax and become totally involved in their learning.

We have to be prepared for a wide range of different weathers during summer as well as through the other seasons. Rain may dominate for a period of time but because it is not as cold as winter rain, there may be different ways children can become involved in experiencing the rain and have longer periods outside in wet weather.

It is important to remember that if the sun comes out, even for a short time, it can be very intense and children need to be well protected.

Parents can be asked to provide sun hats and cream. Young children need to be placed in the shade and older ones need to be encouraged to find shady places to settle in. Supplies of drinking water should also be readily available, and children reminded to access this frequently. Children need to understand the importance of wearing hats and some children will also need long-sleeve protection.

In this chapter there are indicators of what to look out for in the summer with a focus on wildlife and garden areas. Conversation and ideas of how to extend children's play are followed by lists of additional resources to extend children's experience of summer.

Summer walks and outings

Taking children out for walks on a regular basis encourages familiarity with the neighbourhood environment. Visiting the same park or open space helps children to feel secure and to relax and observe changes to the world around them.

Research your local neighbourhood and note any special events. Inform parents about these and encourage them to take their children out whenever possible. If you are organising a main outing you will need to ensure that there are sufficient health and safety checks and that there is an appropriate ratio of adults to children. If parents are involved in a large outing, it is a good idea to talk to them first in a group and as well as outlining safety procedures. Discuss the ways in which they can communicate with children and encourage them to observe and talk about all that they hear and see. Working outdoors with you will give parents a sense of the way they can encourage children to be observant on family outings.

Look out for:

- Grasses and flowering plants.
- Insects and wildlife.

Talk about:

- The sounds you can hear – if you are in a wood it might be birdsong, or in a meadow the chirping of grasshoppers or leaves rustling in the breeze.
- The colours of summer – bright colours of flowers; colours and patterns on insects.
- The dappled light coming through trees.
- Different shades of green.

Supply:

- Mobile phone, first-aid kit, any necessary health and safety paperwork, contact numbers.
- Camera.
- Bags for children to collect things to take back to the setting.

Case study

Sharing experiences with children – a family outing in the summer

Harry had been on a fairly long walk that included lots of chances to climb trees and run up narrow paths. On the way home he picked up a holly leaf and asked:

Why is this leaf prickly?
    G. explained that it was a defence against being eaten by squirrels or cows. Harry understood about defences from his Star Wars and Skylander play.

G: It's all to do with plant defence – to stop animals eating their leaves. Lots of plants have defences – like nettles which sting.
H: I have to find a long leaf if I get stung.
G: Some plants have poisonous berries; some trees have sharp thorns. (Points to juniper bush.)
H: I could get prickled if I touched one of those.
G: Let's find some hawthorn berries. Look, these berries have got seeds inside – they will grow to make new plants and then here are some nuts that the squirrels like to eat.
H: What other seeds are there?
G: There are all these grass seeds. If you pull them off like this, you can get a handful and blow them away like the wind does.

Harry experiments with blowing grass seeds.

H: I like this sort the best, they go furthest (walks a bit further). Now Grandpa, let's sit down here and talk about the plants – we need to sit down.

H. promptly sat down in the middle of the path and waited for G. to join him.

H: Those stinging nettles are dangerous and when people touch them they get stung and they need a thin leaf to make them better. When brambles get you and you push hard on them, you have blood and you have to get a plaster and you don't know where the plasters are cos there's none of them in the forest.
Some months later Harry watched the leaves falling down in the garden
H: Is this winter time?
G: No it's called autumn. It comes before winter.
H: Oh yes, winter is when the tree makes new buds inside.

Harry is a four-year-old who finds it difficult to concentrate on indoor activities. He spends a lot of time in his own imaginary world. When outside, he likes to run and walk for a long way and then he will eventually walk alongside and begin to notice the things around him. He obviously remembers what he has been told and can recall it after a length of time. While outside, he is able to relate to adults and shows a deep interest and awareness of the things around him, but it is important that the adult is able to share this with him.

Sun and shade

Outdoor spaces can be planned to provide shade by planting some trees or large shrubs. A pergola or canopy can be covered with a camouflage cloth until plants have grown over it. Climbing plants that flower and also create shade are honeysuckle and clematis, but both need to be supported on a frame. If you have space for trees, choose a variety that gives colour at different times of year but also offers shade in the summer (see Chapter 3). In a shared space, it may be possible to use some tall bamboos planted in flowerpots. Otherwise work with the children to create dens and shelters. Covers can be placed over A-frames, chairs or tables. It may be possible to attach a ready-made curtain to a wall or fence using the loops at the top. It can be pegged down on the ground and will give a shady space. If you have your own shrubs, try to prune the inside of one so there is space for children to creep inside it and have a private, leafy space. Natural shade will vary through the day and this is a good opportunity to help children become aware of the movement of the earth around the sun and the way shadows shorten and lengthen through the day.

Help children to understand the nature of heat and heat loss. Water placed in different parts of the garden will evaporate at different rates depending on sun or shade.

Look out for:

- Small spaces that can be covered to provide extra protection.
- Shrubs and bushes that can be used for shade.
- Spaces under trees that can be used and made attractive to children.
- The movement of shade through the day.

Talk about:

- The movement of the earth around the sun as children can observe the way the shade moves across the spaces; short shadows at midday become longer as the afternoon goes on.
- Why we need to be in the shade when the sun's rays are strong.
- The light and heat that come from the sun.

Supply:

- Sun hats.
- Sun protection cream (always discuss this with parents and ensure children with any allergies bring their own).
- Long-sleeved shirts if necessary.
- Additional shady spaces made with fabrics and covers.
- Water in different-sized containers in different places – use a dip in the ground if you have one and children can measure the size of the puddle and draw chalk marks at regular intervals to measure the rate of evaporation.

Summer picnics

Eating outside in summertime is always an adventure. There is always the challenge of planning for all kinds of weather, but children will enjoy it whatever the weather. Planned picnics may include invitations to special visitors or parents, and if the children help to prepare the food it becomes even more exciting. It is possible to grow salad crops in very small spaces and it only takes a week for cress to grow. Home-grown tomatoes and strawberries may even be on the menu. If the weather is bad, spread the groundsheet or rug indoors or if you have a tent, a tarpaulin roof or den, children can shelter there while they eat. Helping to plan the picnic and prepare the food gives children experience of organisational thinking, weight and volume, shapes and measuring as they chop food and cut sandwiches.

Imaginary picnics

This will happen all year round, but often if the weather is fine children can relax and settle down for longer periods. A dolls' or teddy bears' picnic may be an organised event or spontaneous role-play generated by the children. Children will include picnic or outdoor mealtimes in their role-play. Dens and shelters may be used or children may find their own spaces, just as a group of boys took their dolls onto a wooden bridge and settled there to feed and care for them. Picnic play can be extended if children can access a wide range of natural materials and use these in their play.

Look out for:

- Salad crops that can be used for sandwiches.
- Fruits to make a summer fruit salad or summer berry shake or ice cream (see recipes in Appendix).
- Suitable spaces and places for picnics (children will often make their own and you may need to just provide some additional shade with a draped curtain).
- Natural materials that can be used to make imaginary meals, e.g. fallen flower petals, grass cuttings, seed heads (dead-heading flowering perennials will produce these), small twigs, old catkins lying on the ground, pieces of bark or wood off-cuts for serving dishes and plates.

Talk about:

- Eating healthy foods.
- Children's ideas for a picnic and what they might need, as well as what they would like to eat.
- Rhymes and stories about outdoor adventures, e.g. *Mr Gumpy's Outing* by John Burningham; *The Lighthouse Keeper's Lunch* by Ronda Armitage.

Supply:

- Rugs and mats.
- Provision for additional summer dens.
- Items to encourage role-play, e.g. a small picnic hamper, small baskets, rucksacks.
- Appropriate food and preparation utensils.

Summer-themed role-play

Many settings are keen to encourage appropriate role-play for the season of summer. Sometimes it is part of the adult planning for the season and sometime it may occur as a natural progression of children's interests. Garden sheds can be resourced as ice-cream stalls and there may be an outdoor space that can be used as a 'beach area'. Small deckchairs and rugs give spaces for conversations and imaginary play. Bats, balls and beach games can also be provided. On a real beach, however, it is the combination of sand and water that keeps children occupied for longer periods. The chapters on earth (Chapter 9) and water (Chapter 11) give more information on setting up a beach area, but if you can offer a water supply near the sandpit and children can take off their socks and shoes, they will be able to become deeply involved as they play.

Talk about:

- Children's own experiences of summer – some may not have been on a beach and others may have experienced cold as well as warm weather on a beach.
- Sand – what it feels like on your hands on your feet. Younger children will probably have already put it into their mouths and soon learn what it tastes like.
- The sea – being mindful of children who may not have experienced this, use a photo or video to help them understand. Encourage parents to tell you if they are planning to go to a beach with their children so you can talk about it on their return.
- Ice-cream stalls – different flavours and ways to serve ice cream; make some real ice cream (see recipe in Appendix).

Many children spend time in this local park where they can access sand and water. Social group play is highly developed as children take turns and work together on complex systems of sand and water trenches.

Supply:

- Sand and water – ideally a large sandpit but otherwise sand in several large containers or builders' trays so children can feel it between their toes.

- A range of containers for the ice-cream stall, materials for children to make decorations for the stall, price lists and advertisements, materials to make 'pretend' ices and lollies.

- Empty sun-cream containers, small deckchairs, beach mats, bags, towels, buckets and spades, sand moulds, beach flags, armbands, old sunglasses, umbrellas, maybe a windbreak.

Keeping cool

Children and adults both need to be aware of the importance of keeping cool if the weather is very warm. A breezy day may give enough natural movement of air, but if it is very sultry fans may be needed. Children may enjoy making their own fans. Water is a cooling element and more ideas can be found in the chapter on water play (Chapter

11). Builders' trays can provide shallow paddling pools, and if you are able to have a safe, fixed water feature, this can provide cooling play as it will have an endless fascination for children.

Talk about:

- Why it is so hot.
- The importance of keeping cool – why and how we can do this.
- The differences in air temperature at different times of day and in different areas, e.g. shaded and exposed.
- Other countries where it is very hot for much of the year – and the reasons for this. What sort of animals live in these countries and how have they adapted? How do animals survive in the desert? What sort of plants survive in hot countries?

Supply:

- An easily accessible supply of drinking water.
- Additional dens and shelters; cool places.
- Outdoor thermometers.
- Water in a variety of containers.
- A deep tray and very large containers for children to just fill, empty, pour and use to splash around.
- Large plastic bottles, bowls, funnels and jugs, stored so children can choose and access easily.
- Large and small umbrellas for shade.

In the garden

Even if you have only a small space, pots and containers can be a mass of colour during the summer. Children enjoy looking closely at flowers and you should be able to attract a range of insects. Watering is often the main activity or if you have had a wet spell, weeding becomes more important.

Plants

If you have sown flower seeds in the spring they should be flowering now. Ornamental and native grasses provide rich habitats. Children can walk amongst them, hide in them and hear them rustling in a summer breeze.

Encourage children to collect fallen petals or seed heads and provide space for storage. If you have a sensory or herb garden, this will come into its own in the summer. Lavenders, marjoram, mint and thyme can be picked regularly. Roses will provide petals for children to use in play.

If you have planted sunflowers they will be growing taller every day. They usually, however, reach their maximum height in the early autumn and the flowers are at their best in September. Children will enjoy measuring them and recording their growth on a regular basis.

July is the ideal time to plant some autumn-flowering bulbs, which will provide colour later in the year. Autumn-flowering crocus can be planted in pots or in beds. *Nerine bowdenii* is a delicate pink flowering bulb and needs good drainage. It likes sandy soil.

Many flowering shrubs are at their best, and the tree canopy is much denser.

Look out for:

- Young birds in the shrubs and trees, maybe still being fed by a parent.
- Flowers on shrubs and trees – if it is possible to pick some without damaging the plant children may use flower heads in their play; many flowering shrubs drop petals every day and these can be collected.
- Eggs laid on the back of a leaf.
- Leaves that have been eaten by caterpillars, snails or insects.

Talk about:

- The increase in growth and the warmth that we feel in the sun.
- The different types of weather and how this affects flowers – watering may be required in dry spells.
- The perfume of flowers and herbs.
- The flavours of herbs and how they are used in cooking; children can use these or take them to the kitchen for use in meals (see curry recipe in Appendix).

Supply:

- Bags, trays or baskets for children to collect fallen petals.
- Small containers for children to arrange flowers and herbs.
- Water and containers for children to make rose-petal perfume, potions and mixes.
- Measuring sticks, string or tape measures to record growth.
- High-quality art materials for children to draw and paint flowers.
- A camera to record growth or take pictures of flowers at different stages.
- Magnifying lenses – children enjoy peering closely into the inside of flowers.

Fruit and vegetables

During the summer months, children will be able to observe the ripening processes as strawberries and tomatoes turn from hard green fruits to juicy red ones. These fruits can be grown in patio pots or growbags. Tomatoes need to be supported by a cane. The small side shoots that appear between the main leaf and the stem should be pinched out to encourage fruits to swell and more flowers to form. One plant should provide five or six clusters of fruits. They benefit from regular watering and children should be involved in this. Strawberries will need protection from birds. Picking and eating fresh strawberries is a memorable experience for children, especially if they have been involved in the planting and caring processes.

Early potatoes may be harvested in the summer. Once the flowers have died back and the leaves appear to have stopped growing, they are ready to harvest. Children will be excited as they discover them in the soil and they will enjoy counting them and sorting them into sizes.

Pea pods are swelling and once the pod is really swollen they can be picked. Peas can be eaten directly from the pod as long they are carefully inspected first.

Broad beans are also ready for picking. One preschool encourages each child to plant a bean and enter it for the local horticultural show. This encourages links with the local community as well as helping children to understand the nature of horticulture.

Salad crops are fairly easy to grow and again should be ready for picking and using now. Lettuces, chives and radishes will grow in any small space or container.

Children at St. Michael's Community Nursery made elderflower cordial after gathering flowers from a nearby tree. They used a recipe from the internet.

Picking and shelling peas is a satisfying experience, and eating them when they are fresh is even better.

Look out for:

- The flowers on plants and continue to observe how the tiny fruits are formed after pollination.
- The growth process, and record this if appropriate.

Talk about:

- The needs of the plants – light, water and warmth.
- The ripening processes.
- The taste and smell of freshly-picked peas or tomatoes.

Supply:

- Small watering cans.
- Child-size garden tools.
- Art materials for children to record plant growth.
- A camera.
- Measuring sticks, both informal and regulated.
- A readily accessible source of water and watering cans.
- Reference books.
- Recipes for children to use produce.

Wildlife

Flying insects

Summer-flowering plants will attract a range of flying insects, butterflies and moths. Lavenders and catmints are very popular so try to have some either in a pot or flowerbed.

Look out for:

- Honey bees, wasps, hoverflies, butterflies, moths, ladybirds, damselflies and dragonflies.

Talk about:

- Bees – the different types of bee and how they work together in a hive to produce honey.
- The need to plant suitable flowers as the bee population is declining.
- Wasps and hoverflies – hoverflies cannot sting and wasps in general should be avoided.
- Butterflies – observe which plants they rest on and remind children of the life cycle and earlier stage, which they may have seen earlier in the year; see if they remember the word 'metamorphosis'.
- Dragonflies and damselflies – these may be observed in many spaces, particularly if there is a small pond nearby. The female lays her eggs on the leaves of water plants and the larvae live in the pond from one to three years before they emerge as adults ready to mate and begin the cycle again.

Ground creatures

If you have created a bug palace, or even left a few old logs in a shady corner, now is the time to see what is hiding there.

Look out for:

- Woodlice, centipedes, millipedes, earthworms, spiders, earwigs, slugs and snails.
- Ants' nests, which may be found in the soil or under a disused flowerpot.

Suitable clothing allows children from an early age to discover and connect with the natural world throughout the seasons.

Members of staff have encouraged parents to take their toddlers to forest school sessions and have helped them to construct a wooden xylophone!

Children learn about the development of new shoots as they plant these early potatoes in a large container.

These children are carefully watering their seedlings in early spring as the weather has been dry.

Caring for wildlife is very important. This group is feeding the birds near their nest box, which contains a video camera. They then enjoy watching the birds fly in and out of the nest as they feed.

Children have swept up cherry blossom and transported it in containers to play with in different ways.

Summer prunings of large shrubs can be used to encourage den-making.

A supply of covers of different shapes and sizes plus some large pegs encourage children to think about how they can construct their own hiding places.

These children are making hiding places for wildlife as they construct an elaborate 'bug palace'.

Children from this nursery visit a nearby allotment and learn a lot about looking after vegetable crops.

Children are fascinated by sand on a large scale. A sand pit is essential if you have your own outdoor space and it should be as large and as deep as possible.

A nearby rainwater tank enables children to help themselves to water to fill their channels. This is an excellent way to extend sand play, particularly in the summer months.

Sun hats are essential when it is hot and so is the important task of weeding the nursery vegetable plot.

Children enjoy harvesting produce. Here, elderflowers are being used to make a summer fruit cordial.

The cherry tree that provided so much spring blossom now provides more fun as the children enjoy playing in the autumn leaves.

Even very young children are fascinated by autumn leaves and enjoy the experiences they offer.

Children have helped to cut up ingredients which have been chosen to reflect the colours of the flames and enjoy taking turns to stir the 'bonfire soup'.

A small green caterpillar fascinated the children, particularly as it was the autumn so they did not expect to find one.

Collecting conkers is a memorable childhood experience. Parents and grandparents can often take children out to do this if there are no conkers near the early years setting.

Digging up autumn potatoes helps children to understand the reasons for growing food as well as developing mathematical thinking as they count and sort for size.

Very young children become confident learners as they share winter experiences with an adult.

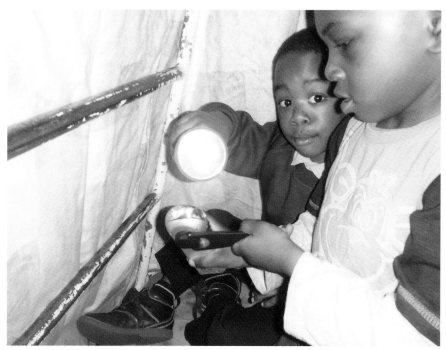

Winter gives us an opportunity to offer experience of dark places, and children love to use torches especially in their own secret den.

Paint mixing takes on a new meaning as children experiment using snow.

Sub-zero temperatures did not prevent children writing letters to the giant to tell him where to find his hand (see Case Study: 'Ice' in Chapter 8).

After an initial investment in good quality rain gear, it costs very little to allow children to have exciting experiences in rain and mud – just some plastic bottles and maybe a few sheets of paper.

Instead of sweeping away this very large puddle, children extended play over several days adding bridges, boats and fishing lines, and learnt about balance, floating and sinking as well as splashing.

Children quickly become deeply involved with the natural world – making a collection encourages imagination. This girl is building a home for a woodland fairy as part of her forest school session.

Having a special place to set out collected things encourages creativity and mathematical thinking in children.

Toddlers love nothing more than exploring mud. Parents and children shared the fun of cleaning the wellies after this session (see Case study: Treetots in Chapter 4).

A large, deep container or tray filled with soil and water, together with some cooking utensils, allows children to become deeply involved in mud play.

Large fir cones make an interesting alternative to a paint brush. In this nursery children use a wide variety of natural objects, paints and colours to develop creativity.

Toasting marshmallows on an open fire is an experience these children will remember for a very long time. Parents and staff are aware of the need for careful safety management but also the importance of this type of outdoor experience.

Talk about:

- Why we need to handle any creatures with care and put them back in the right environment.
- The patterns on snail shells – they are not all the same.
- How different creatures move – particularly if they don't have legs, e.g. worms, slugs and snails.
- The slimy trail left by snails and slugs.
- Which creatures are insects (insects have three pairs of legs, a pair of antenna and a three-part body: head, thorax and abdomen); children will love to learn these new words.
- That the woodlouse is a crustacean and has 14 segments to its shell.

Supply:

- Magnifiers and lenses.
- Pooters and a range of small containers.
- Paper with powdered graphite sprinkled on and left out overnight, which will record snail trails.
- A camera.
- Drawing materials.
- Reference books, identification charts and websites (www.a-z-animals.com; www.insects.org; www.jennywiggins.com; the latter is an artist's website showing snail drawings and landscape art).

Conclusion

Our experiences of summer will inevitably vary from year to year depending on the weather. We may be lucky enough to have a perfect summer's day with a gentle breeze and lots of sunshine. Make the most of these, as they are sometimes few and far between. Many days are a mixture of weather so we need to be prepared to be flexible. A garden can present its own challenges, either needing lots of watering, or when there is a lot of rain it will need more weeding. Hopefully, your care will be rewarded and children can benefit from the satisfaction of picking their own flowers, fruits and vegetables.

Further resources

Summer art

Posters and prints of the following may be bought from www.allposters.co.uk:

At the Beach by Edward Henry Potshard.
Summer Landscape by Pierre-Auguste Renoir.
A picture showing a profusion of wild flowers.
Summer Fun by Kirsten Ulv.
A print of beach items – ball, sunglasses, flipflops and a shell; good for discussion.

Paintings by Claude Monet at www.claudemonetgallery.org:

The Artist's Garden at Giverny (c. 1900).
A rich tapestry of colour.

The Sailboat.
Encourage children to look closely at the way the light shines down.

The Beach at Etretat.
The Beach at Pourville.
Bouquet of Gladioli, Lilies and Daisies.

Summer music

Summertime by George Gershwin.
'Summer' from *The Four Seasons* by Vivaldi.
Midsummer Night's Dream by Mendelssohn.
Classical Summer CD by the London Symphony Orchestra, available from Amazon.
Summer Holiday by Cliff Richard.

Summer stories

A Day at the Seaside by Penny Thompson (Campbell Books 1989).
Brambly Hedge: Summer Story by Jill Barklem (Harper Collins 1999).
Maisy at the Beach by Lucy Cousins (Walker 2002).
Oliver's Fruit Salad by Vivian French, illus. Alison Bartlett (Hodder Children's Books 1998).
Oliver's Vegetables by Vivian French, illus. Alison Bartlett (Hodder Children's Books 1995).
The Big Big Sea by Martin Waddell (Walker 2009).

Summer reference books

Butterflies by Gallimard Jeunesse and Claude Delafosse (Scholastic First Discovery 2007).

Nocturnal Animals by Mary Dunn (Capstone Press 2011).

The Deep Blue Sea – An Ocean Wildlife Book by Jakki Wood (Frances Lincoln 2006).

Ready Steady Grow by RHS (Dorling Kindersley 2010).

www.uksafari.com has sections and identification charts for all types of wildlife and flowers.

7 | Autumn

Introduction

Autumn is the time when we think immediately of changing colours and ripe fruits. The season begins around the 21st September and there is a mellow feel about the warm days that often occur. Garden flowers are still colourful and the warm sun sharpens the intensity of the changes in the leaves and flowers. There may also be days of gusty winds and rain. The days then get noticeably shorter and animals and plants begin to prepare for winter. Talk to other adults in the nursery about your childhood memories of autumn as well as your feelings about the season. By sharing your feelings with the children, you will encourage them to examine their own attitudes and develop self-awareness.

If your outdoor space has been carefully planned and includes some trees and shrubs chosen for autumn colour, children will experience the changing colours of leaves. Alternatively, you may be able to take them to a local park or garden to observe the changes. Going for walks in the autumn is particularly exciting if you have a woodland space. Children will always find something special to pick up to take home, so always take a bag. This chapter suggests what you might find on an autumn walk as well as how to make the most of the autumn colours and leaves.

Autumn walks

Whether you are in a city or in the country it is always possible to find somewhere to go where children can crunch though leaves, maybe collect conkers or other fruits and stand under a tree as the leaves blow down around them. Although the following case study is about walking in woods it will give ideas on what to look for and how to encourage children to discuss and think about what they find.

These leaves were collected at the start of an autumn walk and laid out on the ground so that children could discuss their size and shape.

Case study

Walking through woods in autumn

At Peter Pan Preschool Nursery, children go out into the woods on a regular basis. Today a group of eight children led by J., a staff member who is also a forest school practitioner, a parent helper and an observer, set off for a two-hour session in woodland. Children all dressed in wellies and waterproof trousers and coats. The first part of the session consisted of a walk through nearby woods. On the edge of the wood they ran to collect leaves and brought them back to J. She asked them to line them up and together they discussed which leaves were bigger, and then ordered them by size. They also looked closely at the shapes and colours in the leaves and any other markings. J. explained that there was no chlorophyll left at this time of year and as it broke down other colours were revealed. One of the children said it was because it was autumn. As they entered a grassy glade, one child spotted a spider's web shining with dew in the sunshine. Other children gathered round and one asked, 'Where is the spider?' A few children thought he had gone, but one noticed that he was very small and was on the side of the web.

Look, look, he's waiting for a fly

Another child: He's asleep.

This led to children finding another web with a fly in it, and a conversation about dinner and the other types of food a spider liked.

Children followed along the path and one spotted a small, brown toadstool. Another child saw a red one. This was fly agaric: a poisonous variety. J. used a small stick to point it out to the children and warned them that they should never touch or damage any fungus as it could make them very ill. She also explained that when they died down they helped the goodness come back into the soil. (Reference guides are kept at the nursery for children to identify anything they find.)

Further along the path J. pointed out the decaying fronds of bracken, held one up and pointed out it was even taller than her.

Two children noticed a bramble plant and didn't want to touch it but needed to go past it. 'It is really sharp and spiky, it might hurt me.' J. showed the children how to use their bodies and feet to get past safely without using their hands. On the way back along the track children would stop to pick up a special leaf, stick or something that caught their eye. These had to be carefully put away so they could go back to nursery and then be taken home. Children also found large, waxy leaves from a specimen tree and used them as pretend umbrellas. They all wanted one to take back to the nursery and these were carefully stowed in a wheeled storage box that the children pulled along with two ropes – named 'Trundle Dog'. The children then went into a part of the woods that was used for a forest school session. They knew the rules about boundaries and also were practising safe sitting in front of a campfire space in preparation for a session that involved lighting the fire. Some children explored a raft of logs that led to an island. They had to negotiate how to climb across using hands and feet, managing their own risk. Water had gathered on one side of the logs since the last visit and the children noticed this and used it in their play.

Two children picked up long sticks and used them as fishing rods: 'I'm going to catch a shark.' They later decided to invent a rowing boat and the sticks became the boat and they wanted a passenger. The girls were busy making a bedroom out of bracken in the log den they had built the previous week and were not interested in joining the boys, so I clambered in and we went off to a station. After this some boys came over to the den and were sent off to find some more fish to cook. Two girls built a fireplace using sticks and leaves. They added different types of imaginary food to be cooked and taken into the den to eat. One child found a small caterpillar on a log and watched to see if it moved: 'I think he's going to go down that hole'.

Boys were challenged as they climbed over this log raft. Girls were playing in the den behind and came over later to join them.

The session ended with a game of hide-and-seek, and then a hot drink and a snack under a tarpaulin round the campfire circle. Children watched the patterns of leaves on the roof and noticed the tall trees swaying in the wind. Children were not really ready to go back as they were enjoying themselves so much and the time had passed very quickly.

This case study clearly shows the three types of learning discussed in the introductory paragraph to Chapter 1 (Characteristics of effective learning). Sensory or experiential learning was evident as children noticed the sunlight streaming through the trees and the leaves blowing down in the wind. They had first-hand experience of change in the environment, noticing the presence of water. They experienced wet grass, brambles, slippery logs and moss, the damp smell of the woods in autumn, the sound of the robin, and the taste of hot chocolate. Acquisition of knowledge was evident in the conversations and interactions between the children and the adults and between the children themselves.

Children managed their own risk as they negotiated brambles and climbed across sticks and logs. Different areas of the curriculum were covered in an exciting and spontaneous way using natural materials as reference points. Creative and child-initiated learning was the foundation for the imaginative play and, at the same time, this was supporting the development of physical and social skills as children played together and negotiated roles and responsibilities. Having free time in the open space allowed them to play and make discoveries for themselves, allowing a deeper level of involvement. It is also evident that children benefit from revisiting the same space on a regular basis and developing play over time. Adults modelled how to behave when outdoors and, using a stick to point out the fungus, reinforced the message that it should not be touched by hand.

Children between three and five are able to spend long periods of time in purposeful play without any man-made equipment or expensive resources. The concept of 'affordance' as defined by James Gibson (1986) stresses how natural objects can be imbued with a vast variety of uses. A stick can be a fishing rod, a piece of food, a drawing utensil, a piece of cutlery and so on. A plastic real-life object cannot be used in this way. Good clothing, a waterproof tarpaulin shelter, a first-aid kit, mobile phone, snacks and drinks are the main requirements.

Autumn leaves

There are several plants that give good autumn colour and are suitable for nursery outdoor spaces. Ornamental cherry trees and Japanese acers are amongst the most common. Try to find some trees nearby where children can walk through leaves, as well as observe the changes in colour. Ask parents if, when they take children out for a walk, they could collect leaves of different sizes and shapes. A walk in an arboretum or garden will afford the opportunity to see a wide range of species.

Babies and toddlers will enjoy crawling or walking through fallen leaves and young children and adults should walk through leaves and have fun together.

Leaves can be gathered in several ways and used for different activities. Older children may want to make a collecting wand. A long stick can be used to gather leaves by threading them on to it and then holding it up to the light to examine the veins.

Younger children enjoy filling any container with leaves – boxes, bags or wheelbarrows. If leaves are pressed they can be used for making collages, leafy shapes, leafy creatures, cards and bookmarks. Encourage children to collect different sizes and shapes. On return to the setting try to press some leaves as this means that they will last better if used for decorative purposes. To do this, lay the leaves on a sheet of newspaper, leaving a space between each leaf. Place another sheet of newspaper on top and put some heavy books on them. Leave for a few days before using them. Leaf painting, leaf printing and leaf rubbing are all popular activities at this time of year. Children may also enjoy taking photographs of trees and leaves, and then comparing them to photographs taken earlier in the year. Pressing leaves helps them to stay flat and is useful if children want to make art pictures with them. They need to be dried with kitchen paper and then spread out on newspaper so they don't touch each other. Place another sheet of newspaper on top, together with a heavy weight such as books and leave for a few days.

Look out for:

- Leaves of different shapes, sizes and colours.
- The veins in the leaves and different patterns.
- Leaves that are still on the trees.
- Leaves on the ground – babies and toddlers will enjoy crawling or walking through fallen leaves and young children and adults should walk through leaves together.
- Safe, clean places where children can pick up and throw the leaves.

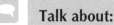

Talk about:

- Why the leaves are changing, what makes them change, why some leaves stay on the trees all year; use the words 'evergreen' and 'deciduous'.
- Shades as well as colours – flame, scarlet, amber, lime, russet.
- Sounds that are made as you walk – scrunching, scuffling. Can you hear the leaves rustling on the trees?
- Different shapes and sizes of leaves – compare the veins in the leaves with the veins in your hands.

Supply:

- Paints of different autumn shades for younger children so they can make finger prints or paint large leaves.
- Paints that older children can mix themselves with a range of thick and thin brushes.
- Fine felt-tips or crayons in a range of autumn shades for free drawing.
- Paper, glue and card for children to make pictures using pressed leaves (leaves of different sizes and shapes can be used to create fantasy creatures as well as shapes and patterns; wax crayons or cobblers wax can be used for leaf rubbings; clay can be used for leaf prints, dried out and painted).
- Frames and string or wool for children to weave an autumn collage.
- Containers for children to collect leaves; boxes, bags, wheelbarrows and small trucks for toddlers.
- Space on the ground for children to make leaf patterns or pictures.
- Musical instruments for children to use to imitate leaves falling to the ground.
- A digital camera for children to use to take close-ups as well as long-distance photos of trees and leaves.

Autumn fruits in the wild

Encourage parents and children to observe shrubs and trees closely. Mixed hedges can be seen in towns as well as in the country, and they often provide a food source for birds. You may even have a hedge on your own boundary.

Look out for:

- Acorns, conkers, beech mast, sweet chestnuts, conkers and sycamore seeds (throw these in the air and watch them spin like little helicopters). Ask parents to collect natural resources with their children if they go out for a walk.
- Berries beginning to form on shrubs and trees – rose hips and hawthorn.
- Squirrels collecting nuts.

Talk about:

- Seed cases – link the fruits with children's experience of seed sowing in spring
- Touch the spiky sweet-chestnut case and compare it with the velvety smoothness of a conker.
- Ripening and harvest – who or what will eat these things?
- Roast sweet chestnuts and discuss why we cannot eat all fruits and berries. Emphasise the importance of not picking and eating wild berries.

Supply:

- Water to soak acorns, so children can observe the beginning of germination.
- Additional storage for collections, so they can be used in role-play and den play as well as a range of other creative activities.
- Sticks and twigs to create picture frames and space for children to make designs with their collections.

Harvesting flowers, fruits and vegetables that children have grown

This will depend on how much growing space you have. Jute bags or large pots can give a good harvest of potatoes and carrots. Pulling carrots and digging up potatoes is really exciting and children are often surprised by this and enjoy counting them as they come up. They can also be sorted for size.

If you have been able to plant some small fruit trees, children may be able to pick apples or pears or watch an adult pick them.

If you have a church near your setting, it may be possible to organise a visit to coincide with harvest festival time. Children could then see a range of produce that has been grown in this country.

If you have grown sunflowers with the children they will be at their best in the early autumn. Children will enjoy observing them and if you have recorded their growth through the summer you will be able to take the final measurements now. As the petals begin to drop the seeds can be collected and roasted. Alternatively, they can be left out to attract birds. Greenfinches and goldfinches, in particular, enjoy them.

Look out for:

- Fruits – blackberries, apples, pears, plums and late tomatoes.
- Vegetables – carrots, potatoes, beans, greens and maybe onions.
- Ripe pumpkins – can be used for soup and pie, seeds can be used for counting, pumpkin can be weighed and measured.

Talk about:

- Which foods need to be cooked, which foods are eaten raw, and which foods can be eaten either way.
- What changes occur as the food is cooked.
- How many ways we can cook and eat potatoes (chips, boiled, mashed, fried, in a salad or even try some chef recipes e.g. dauphinoise potatoes).

Supply:

- Recipes and time to cook produce (make vegetable soup on a cold day to warm children as they play outside).
- Share with parents and ask them to help with cooking any of their favourite dishes.
- Picture books, poems, rhymes and reference books (see list at end of chapter).

In the garden

Planting bulbs

September is the best time to plant daffodils, but tulips and alliums can be planted through October and November. Bulb planting can be done as a group activity using containers and then the bulbs can be planted outside in a garden space after flowering. Alternatively, if you have a large growing space they can be planted straight into the ground or in raised beds. Daffodils should be nearer the back or higher up if younger children are using the space, as they are poisonous if eaten.

Look out for:

- Bulbs of different shapes and sizes.
- Photographs of relevant plants so children understand the time process.

Talk about:

- The scaly outside of a bulb – what it feels like, which way up it should be planted, how many bulbs you are planting ('We started with ten in the packet. We have planted four. How many are left?').
- Whether we can make a hole and put the bulb in it; why we need to cover it up; what the bulb needs to grow; what happens first. Show children where the roots start to form.

Supply:

- Suitable containers and bulbs of different varieties – ideally, children can choose some on an outing to a garden centre or help to order them online.
- Compost, small trowels, watering can.
- Writing materials and plant labels.
- Good quality drawing materials for children who wish to record the process.
- A digital camera.

Making a compost heap and tidying up

Children love to sweep up autumn leaves and they can help gather them to make leaf mould or compost. If you have a special compost bin they can go in there. Alternatively, they can go into a polythene bag, moistened, sealed and then left for a few months. In spring, this will provide leaf mould, which can be added to vegetable and flower plots. Other garden waste that will rot down easily can be added to a compost bin. Vegetable peelings should also be added to this. Children can help to find worms to add to the bin, as they help to aerate and mix the compost.

Look out for:

- Decaying wood.
- Old plants and weeds that can be dug up.
- Fungus growing on logs or in damp areas.

Talk about:

- Why the leaves are falling and what we can do with them.
- Why recycled plant material is good for the soil.
- The importance of **never touching** any fungus, mushrooms or toadstools.
- The way fungi produce spores and help to revitalise the woodland floor for new growth in the spring.

Supply:

- Small brooms and containers for leaves.
- Wheelbarrows and suitable garden tools.

Helping wildlife

If you have a wildlife area with maybe a pond or rotting logs, children will soon realise that there is less wildlife to see than in the summer, although if it is still warm there may be bees and late butterflies. If space is limited, try to make a permanent pile of old logs and twigs in a small corner, or open a bag of compost on the ground and put a few logs on top. After a few days examine it and you may be surprised at how many creatures are moving into winter quarters.

Look out for:

- Sleepy insects and small froglets hiding under logs and in damp leaves.
- Birds collecting on wires in preparation to migrate – swallows are the most commonly seen.
- Spiders and their webs – early mornings are good for spotting webs and sometimes they are covered with dew.

Talk about:

- Why some animals hibernate – make a hibernaculum (a home for animals to hibernate) by taking a polythene sheet (about the size of a growbag), placing it in a quiet, sheltered spot outside and covering it with a deep layer of damp grass cuttings and leaves; add a few small logs or twigs to keep the grass in place.
- Where the swallows go – use a world map or globe to discuss different climates and zones of the world.
- Which other birds migrate (tiny birds such as willow warblers and chiff chaff fly huge distances).
- How a spider makes a web, what gets caught in the web, and what shape it is (spiders have three pairs of glands called spinnerets; as they spin out the silk they move away and secrete a special liquid that makes the silk harden).
- Making nests with twigs and leaves and putting them out for birds to shelter during cold spells.

Supply:

- Reference books and websites for children to look at and adults to use to fact find: (www.uksafari.com/spiders.htm; www.first-nature.com/fungi).
- A camera for adult and children to use, e.g. to take photos of webs.

Conclusion

Of all the seasons, autumn is perhaps the most predictable. Often it begins with a few warm sunny days and we are aware we need to make the most of these, as we know there won't be many more. Through October, we are aware of the changes as leaves begin to change colour. By the beginning of November, there are always windy days marked by falling leaves and the desire to play with them and shuffle through them, before eventually tidying them up to make compost for next year. Children will be more aware of the processes of decay and change over time. They will also learn how plants and animals prepare for the winter days ahead.

Further resources

Autumn stories

Autumn: A Collection of Songs Poems and Stories for Young Children edited by Jennifer Aulie and Margaret Meyerkort (Wynstones Press 1999).
Ferdie and the Falling Leaves by Julia Rawlinson (Gullane Children's Books 2007).
Follow the Swallow by Julia Donaldson (Egmont 2002).
A story about seasons and migration, which can also be used in the spring.

Leaf Man by Lois Ehlert (Harcourt Children's Books 2005).
Leaves by David Ezra Stein (Penguin Board Books 2010).
Oliver's Vegetables by Vivienne French, illus. Alison Bartlett (Hodder Children's Books 1995).
Pumpkin Soup by Helen Cooper (Corgi 1999).
Red Leaf Yellow Leaf by Lois Ehlert (Harcourt Children's Books 1991).
Why Do Leaves Change Colour? by Gerda Muller (Collins 1994).

Autumn art

Autumn Garden and *Wheatfield with Sheaves* (c. 1888) by Vincent van Gogh.
Shows stacked sheaves, but also dramatic sky with autumn clouds. Available at: www. allposters.co.uk.

Autumn Leaves (2008) by David Hockney at www.hockneypictures.com.

Autumn music

'Autumn' from *The Four Seasons* by Vivaldi.
Listen to the above piece. Can children hear anything that makes them think of autumn? Encourage children to make up their own tunes using instruments outside.

Use fabrics in autumn shades to back any relevant displays. Provide fabric lengths or pieces in autumn shades for children to use as they make up stories, tunes or dances.

8 Winter

Introduction

By the end of November, the days are short and often dark and we have to remind ourselves that winter hasn't even started! When 21 December eventually arrives, it is almost Christmas and yet the astronomical winter has only just begun. Many people prefer to think of winter as starting on 1 November so the winter solstice falls midway, and this is referred to as the meteorological winter. There are, therefore, several opinions as to when winter officially begins, and it also depends on the country where you live, even if it is in the same hemisphere.

It is probably more difficult for adults to feel enthusiastic about going outside in the winter than in the spring or summer. However, it becomes obvious when we observe the children that they seem to want to go outside just as much. Even young toddlers will point to the garden and communicate their desire to be out. Winter can offer a great variety of different experiences. There may be several days when the sun stays behind the clouds, or there might be a crisp cold day when the sun shines so brightly the trees and bushes seem to come alive again against the backdrop of a brilliant blue sky. Be aware of these changes and point them out to the children as they play outdoors.

Children need fresh air every day and being out in the winter is just as important. Staff in one nursery where they take babies out for a walk every day in the prams and buggies, report that babies sleep and eat better. Going out will also lessen the spread of infectious illnesses.

This chapter includes many ideas for keeping warm and helping children to enjoy the winter season. Ideas for snowy days are included in Chapter 11, as snow can fall in late autumn or in the spring, but ice is included in this chapter as it is more common in winter months. Children can care for wildlife through the winter and there are suggestions on how to do, this together with lists of resources to encourage creativity and literacy.

Winter walks

Going out for a walk on a regular basis ensures children of all ages get fresh air and exercise. It is important to stress this to parents, in the hope that they might be able to take children out at weekends. A paragraph in your brochure or a special leaflet listing the benefits can help. You could also make a display showing nearby places to take children. Look at the National Trust website (www.nationaltrust.org.uk) for ideas and consider local gardens as well as parks and open spaces. Feeding the ducks is always popular with children from a very young age. If you don't have ducks within walking distance, try taking some breadcrumbs to a local park. Sparrows and chaffinches are eager to be fed and you may even see a robin. Walking out from your setting on a regular basis may mean that there are not many different routes but try walking it in reverse. Sometimes it is amazing how different it can appear. Themed walks can also add variety.

It is now possible to buy buggies to seat six children as well as double buggies. Young babies often enjoy riding in a baby carrier or rucksack. They are able to have a different view of the world around them, and although it is not so easy to talk to the baby on your back, other adults walking alongside can chat to them. Although we may feel the need to go for a brisk walk to keep warm, young children do not always cooperate. They stop and stare at all sorts of things. Having time to observe at their own pace is very important. It is therefore sometimes wiser not to attempt to go too far, but looking at the world through the eyes of the child will often reveal all sorts of exciting little things in a relatively short distance.

Case study

A winter walk

One preschool always takes its children up a hill on a quiet road before they get to a footpath. Today someone had poured a bucket of water on the tarmac and it had run down the slope in long streaks. As the temperature was –1 °C., the water had frozen hard into patterns. The children were able to test the slipperiness and walk up the ice trails.

It's like a railway line.

Look I'm skiing!

When they got back to the nursery the children wanted to pour water on their tarmac to see if it would freeze and so extended and incorporated the experience into their own play.

Themed walks

One setting I visited recently set out along the 'yellow brick road'. Staff had put laminated pictures up around the route and this held children's interest as it was part of their on-going topic. On return to the setting, children laid out the pictures in sequence and another group played out the windy scene in their den.

We're Going on a Bear Hunt by Michael Rosen, *The Gruffalo* by Julia Donalson and *Rosie's Walk* by Pat Hutchins are a few of the many stories that could be adapted.

As you walk out with children encourage them to listen to the sounds around them. You could have 'Listening' as a focus at different times of the year and you may be able to record different sounds for each season using a small dictaphone.

A number walk is as easy to organise in the winter as it is at any time of the year. Number plates on cars, house numbers, signs in shop windows and price tags are just a few things to be seen.

Photograph walks

As children become more familiar with walks, you can add variety by taking some photographs of different things on the route, printing them out, maybe laminating them and seeing if children can spot them on the walk.

Start with easy things like a letterbox, traffic lights and a tree. As children become more observant, you can use photographs of close-up features, a particular flower, maybe the bark of a special tree, a winter-flowering shrub, a leaf, a bird feeder in someone's garden or plants growing on a brick wall. This idea could be extended to make a set of photographs of the same trees and plants at different times of year. This will help children to observe and understand the process of the changing seasons and the way in which plants respond.

Seasonal interest can be found in shop windows. Look out for seasonal vegetables. A florist may display Christmas plants followed by winter flowers or a wintry scene. Let children have time to look at windows and note the labels and the contents of the displays. Allow time for discussion on return to your setting.

Look out for:

- Different plants.
- Small creatures – young children will often spot a spider on a wall or a ladybird on the pavement.
- Things to collect – take a small box or bags.
- Ice or frost on plants.
- Seasonal displays in local shops, in particular the greengrocer and the florist.

Talk about:

- Anything and everything you see – the buds on trees, clouds in the sky, the weather, small plants and animals.
- Shop windows and their contents; in particular, those with flowers, plants and food displays.
- People and pets – dogs may be wearing winter coats, too.
- Anything the children chat to you about – very often when out walking, children will initiate conversations about all sorts of things.

Supply:

- A camera and notebook to record features of walks.
- A bag to hold any collected items.
- A first-aid kit and mobile phone for adult use.
- Any references or special resources if you are going on a themed walk.

Keeping warm

Look at the layout of your outdoor space and see how you can encourage children to engage in keeping warm. They need to have room to run and jump. You may be able to vary this by setting out obstacle courses using moveable resources such as cones, hoops and blocks. If you are able to include a tree trunk or logs, children will be able to climb to keep warm.

Rhymes and poems can be used to encourage children to march around like soldiers or jump like frogs. Talk about their circulation and let children feel each other's fingers. Some will have warm hands and some will be cold.

Small bean bags can be placed on a radiator or in a microwave for children to use as hand warmers if they get really cold, and some settings will have warm drinks available in cold weather. Hot soup can be enjoyed indoors or outside. (See recipe in Appendix.)

Look out for:

- Opportunities to add variety to the outdoor space by creating trails and courses.

Talk about:

- Why we need warm clothes.
- Why moving around helps to keep us warm.
- What sort of food is good to eat in winter and why we need hot food.

Supply:

- Spare clothes.
- Old sleeping bags and covers for story spaces and dens.
- Chalk to mark out courses.
- Cones, planks, climbing bars and nets to make obstacle courses and trails.
- Small moveable resources, balls, bats, cones, logs and stones.
- Outdoor thermometers to measure temperature.

Winter celebrations

There are several cultural festivals during the winter months and these often give a focus point for a nursery setting. Diwali occurs in November and children can make sweets and very often staff will use Diwali lights. Consider using your outdoor space and take the celebrations outside. As it gets darker at the end of the day, children can watch the lights outside and will enjoy making a procession.

Christmas decorations can be made to hang outside on shrubs or a small pine tree if you have one. Christmas foliage can be used to make small gifts for parents. Again, try hanging some Christmas lights outside in the garden for a festive feel. Make a special Christmas tree for the birds using the recipe in the Helping wildlife section in this chapter (see page 123).

Chinese New Year provides another opportunity to use the outdoor space in a different way. If you can make a Chinese dragon children will enjoy taking it outside. Use pots of bamboo to hang lanterns on. You may like to use some of your winter crops in a vegetable chow mein to celebrate this festival (see recipe in Appendix).

Supply:

- Pieces of oasis – try sticking them onto small pieces of bark with PVC glue as this makes a good base for Christmas decorations; children can then add small pieces of fir, holly and other leaves.
- Bamboo in containers to hang lanterns on.
- Torches and outdoor lights.
- Recipe cards and ingredients for cooking.

Natural collections

As the weather gets colder, leaves on the ground become dry and shrivelled but can still be used by children in their play, particularly in role-play in an outdoor den. Tree felling is often done in winter and you may find some useful off-cuts that can be used by the children. Otherwise, find someone who can cut some logs into small sections and give these to the children. Moss and lichen are easier to spot as trees become bare and there will still be sycamore and ash keys on the ground, particularly after a windy day.

Look out for:

- Leaves of different shapes and sizes.
- Conkers, acorns and sweet chestnuts – some of these may have split and show signs of new growth or signs of being eaten by a squirrel.
- Pine needles and pine cones.
- Old branches and twigs for children to use in play.
- Winged seeds – plane tree, lime tree, ash and sycamore.

Talk about:

- The process of decay and regrowth.
- Seed dispersal – some seeds drop to the ground and are carried further away by animals and some use the wind to carry them away from the parent tree.
- Using their imagination to build with natural materials – you may like to suggest a home for a spider or a boat for a fairy. Children will then begin to use their own imaginations and this could also lead to creating stories, rhymes and music.

Supply:

- Bags and suitable storage for collections.
- Spaces where children can use these items in their play, e.g. den or role-play area.
- Floor space for building with natural materials.
- Additional items such as string, card and glue so children can use the natural materials in a variety of ways to create their own works of art.
- If the temperature is below freezing, small trays of water with a piece of string attached can be provided for children to make ice mobiles using a variety of natural materials; freeze them overnight and then hang them up on a branch.

Winter dens

Den-making can be done at any time of the year, but in winter it is important to encourage the children to think about making the den more weatherproof and a bit warmer than a summer space. If you have access to bracken, this can be cut by an adult to make a roof. Children can help to attach it. Provide a waterproof ground covering and maybe a warm rug. A tarpaulin can be stretched over a roof to make it more weatherproof.

Look out for:

- Suitable spaces, branches and bracken.

Talk about:

- The need to make it weatherproof and warm.
- What sort of materials will keep the water out.

Supply:

- Rugs.
- Tarpaulin.
- Pieces of fabric and water for children to test water resistance.
- Some cuddly toys – maybe animals who might like to use the den to hibernate, e.g. hedgehog, squirrel, badger.

Frost and ice

When the weather is really cold you may find that there are days without snow but that the ground is hard. Ice is forming on water in puddles and containers and there is a hard frost covering on the plants. Make sure children and adults are aware if there are any slippery patches. Paths to and from buildings need to be kept clear with salt or sand.

Look out for:

- Ice in the water tray and on puddles.
- Ice on larger ponds.
- Ice crystals on plants.
- Frost patterns on leaves – in the mornings it is often possible to observe that half the garden is in shade and remains white whilst the other half quickly reverts back to green when the sun comes out.

Talk about:

- Why the ice has formed and what you need to make ice – demonstrate this by making ice mobiles with water and natural materials (see case study).

- Why some ice is melting – use the words thaw, freeze and melt.

- The dangers of walking on ice on frozen ponds – use photographs or picture that show where the water is not frozen.

Ice mobiles can be frozen overnight and hung on a branch to reflect the winter sunlight.

Supply:

- Moulds for making ice.
- Ice-cream boxes that can be used to make blocks with plastic animals inside – one block can be left outside and a similar block placed indoors; children can observe which animal is freed first and may be able to deduce that is because it is warmer inside.
- Outdoor and indoor thermometers.
- Smaller containers, which can be used to freeze leaves to make ice mobiles.
- Gutters, pipes and water trays, left out with water in them so children can see what happens the next day.
- Large magnifying glasses to examine frost crystals.

Case study

Ice

A prolonged period of bitterly cold weather. Most of the snow seems to have disappeared, but the night-time temperatures are well below freezing and daytime temperatures around zero.

After the registration period J. announces 'I saw something very interesting on my way in this morning. I think it needs some investigation. Does anyone want to come outside with me?'

A group of eight children expressed interest and went to put on winter coats, gloves and hats. Most children had their own, but there was a box of spares just in case. They walked down the path and looked between two logs and found a chunk of ice. When J. picked it up they saw it was an ice hand, but two fingers had broken off. 'Whose hand is this?' Various answers, but the group agreed it was the giant's hand because it was so big.

Child: We need to mend the fingers.
J: How shall we do that? (J. carried it carefully to a nearby table.)
Child: We need some tape.
(Two children fetched a roll of masking tape and tried this, but it did not work.)

Child: We need some glue.
(The white glue worked and the finger stayed on the hand.)

J: What shall we do with it?

Child: We need to stop it melting – we can put it into the sand.

(The children filled two small buckets but the ice hand didn't fit.)

J: I think we need a tray.

(Children filled a tray and carefully covered the hand with sand.)

J: Do you think the giant will come to look for it? How can he find it?

Child: We can write him a letter.

Five children sat down to write to the giant. As they made marks on the paper, one girl was singing, 'We've found your hand, it's in the sand', and another boy was talking to himself about the hand as he wrote: 'I've nearly finished I'm just doing a "t" and I need an envelope.'

One child ran inside to fetch envelopes and the next task was to fold the paper so it would fit inside the envelope. This required a little adult help and the children put their envelopes where they thought the giant might find them.

This is a good example of an open-ended activity initiated by the adult who had frozen the ice in a rubber glove and then hidden it. After the discovery, the activity became child-led as children discussed who it belonged to and how to mend the fingers, what to do with it and then how to contact the giant!

The fact that the fingers had broken was not planned and the adults were surprised that the glue actually stuck the ice together.

Children were writing for a purpose and showed great concentration. The folding activity required mathematical understanding of folding in half and matching the shape to the envelope.

Additional experiences with ice

Ice tray

The water tray had frozen over and staff had placed polar bears, penguins and some figures on the ice. Several children played there for a short time but no one seemed to know how the ice had got there. Then two children used a polar bear figure to bang the ice. Small cracks appeared and got larger. Then an air bubble appeared under the ice and some water could be seen: 'Look it's the water that made the ice.' They continued to break it until they made small pieces. After this, they used water from the rainwater barrels to fill it up to see if they could make it freeze over again.

Children used the polar bears to crack the ice and then observed the air bubbles, gradually realising that the ice was formed from water.

Ice mobiles

Children collected natural materials and placed them in small plastic trays. String was laid across and children helped to pour water into the trays. 'When we come tomorrow we will be able to see what has happened. The water might turn to ice and then we can hang the ice blocks up outside.'

Winter sky

The sky in winter presents us with a backdrop of great variety. We may have several days of grey, heavy cloud and then suddenly a day when the sun is out and the sky is a deep Mediterranean blue. Wind will create fascinating cloud patterns and it is worth spending time with children looking at these and talking about them. As the days get shorter, it gets dark often before some of the children in our care go home. In winter, there are fiery sunsets where the sky takes on an intensity of colour, not often seen in the summer. Watch the sunsets with the children and you may see the sun silhouetted on the horizon as a dark red ball. This is really the only time when you can safely see the shape of the sun.

Winter sky at night is the best time to see stars and planets. It may be easier to do this later at night, so talk to parents about making the most of this opportunity with their children.

Look out for:

- Cloud patterns and shapes in the sky.
- Planes flying high in a clear winter sky and aeroplane trails.
- Trees silhouetted against a bright blue sky.
- Winter sunsets.
- Clear nights when you can see the stars.

Talk about:

- Moving clouds – why they are moving and which way they are going; are they all going the same way?
- The colours of a winter sunset – sky will move through amazing shades of blue, turquoise, pink, crimson, orange, peach, purple, flame.
- Whether the sun is moving down or the earth is moving round.
- Why the stars twinkle – use the nursery rhyme and if possible look at a reference book or website.

Supply:

- A digital camera – children can record sunsets, and use photos to help them recall the shades as they recreate this through different media.
- Watercolours, fine brushes, paint, pastels, chalks and paper of different colours.
- Binoculars or a telescope to look at the stars.
- Reference book, e.g. *Usborne Spotter's Guide: Night Sky* by Nigel Henbest and Stuart Atkinson (Usborne 2006).

Darkness

Winter is a very good time for children to begin thinking about the nature of day and night. Many settings will still be open during twilight and dark during the winter months. This is a good opportunity to be with children outside and explore the environment in a different light. Some children may be afraid of the dark; going outside with friends and having fun is a good way to disperse these fears. Babies will enjoy the visual effects of being out in the dark and looking maybe at fairy lights, different colour lights and moving shadows. Using torches in a den or shelter will stimulate children's imagination and highlight the nature of darkness. If you have tried lighting a fire in daylight hours with children, try it again when it is darker as this gives a sense of excitement and adventure. Maybe you can cook outside in the dark (see Chapter 12). Singing round a campfire will offer a musical experience.

Look out for:

- Shadows in the dark and different levels of darkness according to time and weather.
- Night-flying creatures – different species of moths may be attracted to an outdoor light and you may even hear an owl.
- Solar lights or high visibility tape can be used to mark out special places or boundaries; it may be good to start with a smaller space until children feel confident.

Talk about:

- Evening, dusk and night time – different shades and levels of darkness.
- Using torches and the different ways to make the light current (wind-up torches are more eco-friendly and a source of sustainable power; the light beams – light travels in straight lines and cannot go round corners unless it is reflected by a mirror).
- Creatures that like to come out at night such as badgers, foxes, hedgehogs and cats, and how they can see (cat's eyes is also the name for the lights down the middle of a road that glow in the headlights).
- Lighthouse beams, which flash out in darkness to act as a warning.
- Beacons and flashing lights that act as warnings.

Supply:

- Materials and frames to make dark spaces, dens and shelters.
- Different types of torches, including wind-up ones.
- Unbreakable mirrors.
- A string of fairy lights.
- Solar-powered lights outdoors.
- Glow-in-the-dark balls, wands and rings.
- Glow-in-the-dark/luminous paint.
- Night-vision goggles.
- A book box containing:
  - *Day Light Night Light* by Franklyn Branley (Harper Collins 1998)
  - *What Makes Day and Night* by Franklyn Branley (Harper Collins 2001)
  - *The Owl Who Was Afraid of the Dark* by Jill Tomlinson (Egmont Books 2004)
  - *The Dark Dark Night* by Christina Butler (Little Tiger Press 2008)
  - *Can't You Sleep Little Bear?* by Martin Waddell (Walker Books 2005)

Helping wildlife

At the beginning of the season, check that you have some small corners where animals can shelter or hibernate. You may have made a bug palace earlier in the year. Check that it is still in good condition and clean and dry. Otherwise you can make one or just pile up some logs and pack the gaps with soil, dead leaves, hollow plant stems, moss and grass. This will provide a winter home for hedgehogs, ladybirds and spiders. If you are able to leave pruning your shrubs until the end of winter, you will be providing winter shelter for birds. Nest boxes may also be used as winter shelters. Feeding birds is very important during the winter months and when it is really cold they need a supply of fat in order to survive. Bird feeders need to be filled regularly and also cleaned on a weekly basis.

Look out for:

- Birds – blue tits, great tits, robins and chaffinches are regular visitors to many bird tables; in some areas you may spot redwings and fieldfares in very cold weather as they move into gardens in search of food on their way to Siberia where they breed.
- House spiders usually sitting still in their webs.
- Grey squirrels – frequent winter visitors to bird tables as they are often awake during winter months and do not hibernate for the whole season.
- Hibernating snails, ladybirds and spiders in your insect homes.
- Frogs and toads, which may be found under old flowerpots, in the soil or in a log pile.

Talk about:

- Why we need to feed birds.
- Which animals hibernate and how they survive the winter months.

Supply:

- Bird feeders.
- Recipes on laminated card.
- Supplies of bird food.
- Large pine cones to make an attractive feeder (children can stuff pieces of bread and fruit into the cone and then attach it to a branch).
- Small binoculars and a field guide or chart so that children can match species (you could record how many of each species are seen at once).
- Reference books on hibernation, e.g. *Hibernation* by Anita Ganeri (Heinemann 2006).
- Soft-toy creatures and materials to make houses for them, e.g. a shoebox for a toy hedgehog; these can be decorated with natural materials.

Recipe for bird cake

Ingredients

75g maize meal
bird seed mix or chopped nuts, sunflower seeds or niger seeds
two eggs

Stir the maize and nuts together with some water. Beat the eggs and add to the mixture. Pour into a baking tin and bake for 50 minutes at Gas mark 4, 175°C. Cut slices and place a small amount on a bird table (this prevents rodents) or use it to fill fat feeders.

Alternatively, you can melt lard, mix in breadcrumbs and/or birdseed, pour into small foil containers and hang these up.

In the garden

Grow a variety of shrubs that will provide berries and fruit for birds and some that will flower during winter months. Winter honeysuckle and *Hamamelis* both produce pretty flowers and a strong perfume.

In the vegetable garden, you can harvest leeks and winter is a good time to plant some rhubarb crowns. These can be bought in pots from garden centres and two crowns will give enough rhubarb for all the children to enjoy rhubarb crumble in the summer.

At the end of winter, check any vegetable plots for weeds, and let children help to dig in some compost or leaf mould.

Pruning

Children can help to cut back clematis growth if they can reach, but often it will be too high. If this is left until the end of winter it will provide shelter for small birds. Then all the old growth can be cut off any deciduous varieties that bloom in late summer. If you have any apple trees in the garden they should be pruned in December.

Planting summer bulbs and herbs

Children can help plant summer bulbs in pots or containers, or in beds if the ground is not frozen. Use gladioli, nerines or lilies as they will attract butterflies. Planting snowdrops in the green (i.e. after flowering) should be done at this time of year.

Herbs in small pots can be bought at the end of winter and planted into containers, but they may need some protection in cold, frosty spells.

Look out for:

- Winter flowering shrubs – *viburnum bodnantense*, winter honeysuckle and *Hamamelis*.
- Different textured bark such as oak, beech, acer and silver birch.

Talk about:

- The shape and colour of winter flowers and the twiggy structures of some plants.
- The colours and textures of winter bark – it can be rough, smooth, papery, silky, spiky or lumpy.
- Why some trees keep their leaves through the winter.
- Why plants are not growing and why we need to protect some from the frost.

Supply:

- Containers, compost and bulbs such as small gladioli and lilies (tulips are best planted in November).

Signs of spring

During January it is possible to find indications of spring as the days get slightly longer. Snowdrops are usually the first flower to appear followed by winter crocus. During February and March, as the weather gets warmer, small animals come out of hibernation and bulbs push through the soil. There is a noticeable difference in the length of the days as the sun sets later and birds begin to sing.

Look out for:

- Winter catkins – hazel trees bear the long, yellow catkins known as 'lamb's tails' – they dance in the wind and babies will enjoy watching the movements; furry pussy willow can be found on willow trees; *hazel contorta*, or twisted willow, planted in your space will give good catkins from February onwards.
- Snowdrops – truly the first sign of spring; try to plant as many of these as you can in any containers or small corner.
- Any small insects, spiders or butterflies that may be waking up from hibernation.

Talk about:

- Snowdrops – the delicate white petals and the slender stem.
- The textures of catkins and pussy willow.
- Why the insects are beginning to wake up.

Supply:

- Lenses and magnifiers.
- High quality art materials for children to make observational drawings of these early signs of spring – fine paint brushes and fine, well-sharpened crayons will encourage small detail.

Conclusion

Helping birds and other small creature to survive the winter is an important part of conservation. Children will have first-hand experience of the cold days and nights thereby helping to understand the reasons for our involvement. As winter draws to a close, encourage children to reflect on this and also to be aware of the signs of new life and growth that are just beginning to show. Our care, however, needs to continue into the next season and throughout the year, as part of our responsibility to maintain this wonderful natural world.

Further resources

Winter stories

Brr, A Book of Winter – How Different Animals Survive the Snow by Il Sing Na (Meadowside Children's Books 2010).

Jack Frost by K. Kohara (Macmillan 2010).

One Winter's Day by M. Christina Butler (Little Tiger Press 2006).

The Bear's Winter House by J. Yeoman (Andersen Press 2009).

A story about sharing and friendship set against a background of winter.

The Little Lost Robin by Elizabeth Baguley (Tiger Press 2008).

The Snowy Day by Anna Milbourne (Usborne 2012).

Time to Sleep by Denise Fleming (Henry Holt 2001).

Winter by Gerda Muller (Floris 1994).

Winter Hedgehog by Ann Cartwright (Red Fox 1996).

Winter: A Collection of Songs, Poems and Stories for Young Children edited by Jennifer Aulie and Margaret Meyerkort (Wynstones Press 1999).

Reference books

Animals in Winter: Let's Read and Find Out by Henrietta Bancroft (Collins 1997).

Usborne Spotters Guide: Birds by Peter Holden (Usborne 2006).

Someone Walks By – Wonders of Winter Wildlife by Polly Carson-Voiles (Raven Productions 2008).

Trees by Alistair Fitter and David More (Collins 2006).

Winter: Seasons (Go Facts) by Katy Pike (A&C Black 2006).

Winter – Seasons of the Year by JoAnn Macken (Weekly Reader Early Learning Library 2005).

Winter Trees by Carole Gerber and Leslie Evans (Charlesbridge Publishing US 2008).

Winter art

The following prints can be obtained from www.allposters.co.uk:

Starry Night by Vincent van Gogh (1889).

The Woods in Silver and Gold by Anders Andersen-Lundby (c. 1888).

Winter Tunnel with Snow by David Hockney (2006).

Winter music

The Snowman by Howard Blake.

Music books also available for flute and piano arrangements, plus various CDs and also video.

Winter Dreams – Classical Music for When Snow Falls.
A selection of 'winter' classical music by various composers on the Delta label (includes 'Winter' from *The Four Seasons* by Antonio Vivaldi).

General books about the seasons

A Year in Percy's Park by Nick Butterworth (Harper Collins Children's Books 1995).
The Little Book of the Seasons by L. Thornton and P. Brunton (Featherstone Education 2005).
The Little Book of All Through the Year by Lorraine Frankish (A&C Black 2009).

Additional websites for use in settings or at home

www.woodlandtrust.org.uk
Download the leaflets 'Playing through the seasons' – one for each season.

www.forestry.gov.uk
Search for 'places to go' or watch a wildlife video.

www.naturedetectives.org.uk
Good ideas for family activities and nature walks; also has identification charts.

Part 3 The four elements

Much has been written recently about reconnecting with nature. Children are suffering from nature deficit disorder and organisations are beginning to sponsor research into this. As well as tuning into the four seasons, children need to reconnect with the four basic elements of earth, air, water and fire. They can do this simply by being outside on a daily basis and interacting with adults who are able to utilise the elements in such a way that they become an essential part of the child's outdoor learning experience. Earth, air, water and fire offer different experiences, and with some additional resources children will be able to connect in a very real way with each element. The next four chapters explore how the natural elements can be used in early years settings to maximise children's outdoor learning experiences. Each chapter concludes with details of additional learning resources. There are suggestions for extending play and allowing children time and space to explore at a deep level and have fun.

Children will become deeply involved with the elements through playing freely
with sticks and mud

9 | Earth

Using the natural materials offered by the earth, children have a chance to build up the very primeval connection that we are in danger of losing. Observing young children playing with sand and mud enables us to see just how deeply involved they become. A normally active two-year-old can spend a long time just poking around with a stick in some squelchy mud, whilst three-year-olds in a sandpit begin to show a depth of imagination as they create cakes, pies, buildings and road networks.

Mud play

Mud, mud, glorious mud! There really is 'nothing quite like it for cooling the blood'. In the words of the well-known song, the instant appeal is captured in a few easy-to-remember phrases, but the wisdom of these words is much deeper. The word 'cooling' emphasises the calming, relaxing, therapeutic properties of mud. It has been used in therapies across the world since ancient times. So why are we reluctant to let children get out and do what they do naturally? By the age of three, some children are already wary of becoming deeply involved in muddy play for fear of recrimination about getting dirty, or maybe they now don't like getting messy.

The first essential in any setting is for adults to discuss their own feelings about it. Some may recall days in their own childhood when they were able to make mud pies or splash in puddles. Others may feel that it is dirty and the mess is just not worth the effort. Getting messy, however, is an important part of childhood. Children need to be able to manipulate their own environments, to take control of the materials and become involved at a deeper level and for a prolonged period of time.

Hopefully, adults in your setting will be able to work through any barriers and at least experiment with this natural material and then observe the children's reactions. It will, however, need careful planning and resourcing.

Mud play can happen at any time of year and different experiences can be offered at different times. If your setting has a naturally muddy space, children will tend to explore this in winter months. Children need to know they should wear wellies and splash suits before venturing into the muddy area.

Winter and spring
Babies and toddlers

A natural muddy patch with some rainwater in it will keep toddlers involved for long periods of time. Waterproof all-in-one suits or over-trousers and wellies are essential. Toddlers learn how to stamp and splash and will often spend a long time running in and out of the space. Adult support may be needed to give reassurance and encouragement when children first go out into mud. If you have no natural muddy place, create a mud world in an old plastic sheet or tyre on the ground or in a plastic container or old sink.

Threes to fives

Sticks provide a useful tool for exploring and making marks in the mud. Observe how children use these and by adding additional resources you should be able to extend the play. Wooden spoons and some containers, pieces of bark and pine cones can be made available. Older children may wish to write letters in the mud or create patterns using other materials. They may want to make footprints, so think about whether there is a nearby path they could use or alternatively a large sheet of wallpaper or plastic sheeting.

Have a bowl of clean water nearby for children to clean items at the end of play and to rinse their hands before going back inside. A piece of plastic floor covering at the entrance to the building and some chairs will help children to take their wellies off independently before going back in.

Summer

If the same patch becomes muddy in the summer, maybe after a heavy summer shower, consider letting children of all ages access it without shoes and wearing old light clothing. Encourage them to feel the mud squelching between their toes and talk about it. Try using different parts of the foot to make different marks. Provide a roll of old wallpaper for children to make muddy footprints and handprints.

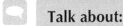

Talk about:

- What happens to the mud when the sun comes out and how it feels then; encourage children to think about the relationship between heat and evaporation.

Supply:

- Bark chips, sticks and twigs, fir cones, catkins and dried seed heads to encourage imaginative play.

Summer mud spaces

Even if you have no natural muddy area, it is possible for children to create their own and it is a good idea to set this activity up in addition to a muddy puddle. Use a large container such as an old wheelbarrow, a builder's tray or a flat plastic sheet in a hollow on the ground. Water can be supplied in a plastic camping water carrier. These are inexpensive and have a small tap which even very young children will learn how to use (though sometimes they forget to turn it off). Use any type of garden soil and let children add their own water from the camping carrier, using small jugs or watering cans.

Children will become absorbed in this play and it may take all sorts of different directions. They may want to splash and make footprints on the sheet on the ground. If the mud is in a deeper container, they may start to make mud pies, or mud cakes, stews or tea. Very often they will want to share recipes with friends. Adults may be able to provide recipe cards and help children to write down their recipe.

Autumn

Mud play in the autumn can be enhanced by the addition of different kinds of autumn leaves and autumn fruits. Conkers, sycamore heads and chestnuts will add variety to children's concoctions.

A mud centre

If you have your own reasonably sized outdoor area, consider providing a permanent mud centre or mud kitchen. It may be a naturally muddy space, but it is often easier to use a convenient space and let children mix their own mud from garden soil or compost and water. It may also be created in a large deep tray. An old cooker and real pots and pans with easily accessible storage will provide a constant source of varied play opportunities for all ages. A range of cooking utensils can be stored nearby and there should be a bucket or a source of water to clean these at the end of a session.

Supply:

- A play cooker with an oven (this can be made out of an old cardboard box reinforced with parcel tape) or an old real one.
- A play or real sink.
- Real cooking utensils {en} colander, sieve, potato masher, large spoons ladle, spatulas (try a jumble sale or car boot sale).
- A small table covered with vinyl cloth.
- Real saucepans, cake and pie tins, plates.
- Bottles of coloured water or paint for children to add colour to their creations.
- Waterproof aprons.
- An old bucket for discarded creations so they do not spoil the main play space.
- An extra bucket of clean, soapy water for children to wash utensils in.
- Storage shelf or pots for utensils.
- A clipboard, card and writing materials to scribe their recipes.
- Small-world creatures such as dinosaurs.
- Builders' vehicles – trucks, diggers and bulldozers if you have a large enough space.

Natural resources

Children will enjoy using a range of natural materials to mix in and to decorate their mud creations. They can collect pine needles, grass, leaves of different shapes and colours, pine cones, reeds and twigs. You may also be able to supply sawdust, bark chips, shells, gravel or small pebbles, flower blossom, crushed eggshells and bottles of different coloured water (coloured with food colouring).

A deep tray, old kitchen utensils, water and soil will keep children purposefully engaged in active and creative play.

Using earth, large pebbles and large leaves, Harry created a house for his dinosaurs and was deeply involved for a long period of time.

Parent partnership

- Send a letter to parents to explain why you are setting up a mud centre.
- Ask them to supply wellies and any spare clothes if you need them.
- Use photographs of children enjoying the mud to make a display.
- Set out curriculum links for parents to follow.
- Encourage parents to let children get messy at home.

Sand play

It is generally agreed that sand play is good for children, but despite this there are still many settings where the only sand is in a shallow plastic tray with a few assorted scoops and shovels. Sand play is not only good for children, but it is an essential resource and can be developed to offer a rich, deeply satisfying, emotional, physical and creative experience. Children need to experience wet and dry sand, and providing sand outdoors enables high quality provision even in a small space. Careful observation of children playing in a well resourced sand area will show that learning is taking place in all areas of development.

Settings with small or shared spaces

Try to offer sand in as deep a container as possible. Provide a table next to it so children can place their creations on it and thus extend play. Wet sand gives children opportunities to dig, mould and build. Dry sand gives opportunities for pouring, sieving, filling and emptying. A wheeled trolley with a variety of suitable containers should also be available. Small funnels, jugs and empty plastic bottles are a useful resource.

Individual deep trays such as pet litter trays can be used to vary this activity. Fill them with dry sand and provide a range of mini containers (hotel shampoo bottles are good, particularly with mini funnels).

Sandpits

In a permanent outdoor space, try to provide a sandpit that is large enough for children to climb in. If you have a wide age range of children it is often a good idea to have two sandpits, maybe a smaller one for toddlers and babies and a larger one for older children. They often want to play collaboratively and play can be sustained over long periods of time. Children need to experience sand with their whole bodies and should have access to sand throughout the year.

Winter

If the sand becomes frozen children may need to use garden trowels or simply discuss why they can't dig the sand and discover how they can use it in a different way, maybe as a hard surface for cars and builders' vehicles. A small toy cooker or a cardboard box set up as a cooker will encourage children to make sand cakes. Children enjoy using real utensils in the sand and small cake tins encourage mathematical thinking as they can make cakes in rows of three or four.

Spring

As it becomes warmer, children may be able to spend longer periods of time handling the sand. If the condition of the sand has deteriorated or the levels have become low, this is a good time to clean the sand and top up the levels. The sand may dry out in the warmer weather and children can use it in different ways. They may like to pour it as well as mould it. Place a flat surface near the sand tray or sandpit or even a plank across it so they can set out tins and containers to fill up for imaginary shops or tea parties.

Summer

If the sand becomes very dry this is a wonderful opportunity to mix it with water. Ideally, children should be able to access a water supply independently, maybe a rainwater barrel. Using buckets jugs or watering cans, they can create channels and trenches in a large sandpit. Even in a plastic sand tray or builder's tray, children enjoy combining the two elements.

Some children may not have visited a beach and had the childhood experience of working and playing with sand and sea. Try to offer something as near to this as possible. The addition of pebbles and shells can help and some settings use seaweed as an additional resource.

Autumn

The sand area may need some protection from falling leaves at this time of year. If leaves are left in the sandpit, they will rot and make the sand dirty. Children will use the sandpit throughout the year and may help themselves to conkers or fir cones as they play. Occasionally these may need to be removed as they begin to rot down. A fresh supply will stimulate play throughout the year.

Supply:

- A range of buckets, rakes and spades, plus large cooking utensils such as ladles, fish slices, colanders and serving spoons.
- Old cake tins, saucepans and frying pans.
- A flat surface and a pretend oven.

Stories to use

We're Going on a Bear Hunt by Michael Rosen (Walker Books 2007).
Mrs. Wishy Washy's Farm by Joy Cowley (Penguin USA 2006).

Conclusion

Earth has been one of mankind's basic play resources for many centuries and even now, children who have little else often use the ground as a play resource. They invent games with stones and pebbles or simply use a stick to scratch around, move earth and make patterns and pictures. Our children are fortunate to have many more resources, but this is one is readily available and can be used to great advantage. Using your imagination and resourcefulness, you will be able to extend children's play appropriately and offer them hours of deep involvement and fun.

Further resources

www.muddyfaces.co.uk
Excellent online resource with information and stunning pictures on mud play and mud kitchens.

10 | Air

It is difficult for children to grasp the concept that air is all around us as they cannot see it. However, even young babies can feel the movement of air as the breeze blows on their skin or ruffles their hair. They will watch moving branches, leaves and hangings mobiles. They will listen to the sound of rustling leaves in a breeze. Older children will experiment with the movement of air as they blow through straws or pipes to make noises and watch things move. They can blow paint across paper or make bubbles out of soapy water. Bubbles rise and are carried away by the wind.

Wind

'Why do kites fly?' This was a question suddenly posed by my four-year-old grandson and I was challenged as I tried to give an answer that was correct and which he would understand. I realised I had never really thought about or understood what made the wind blow, despite having grown up in a windy seaside town.

Young children constantly ask questions in their search for knowledge as they begin to absorb more abstract concepts into their learning. Children need to experience the movement of air in order to understand the nature of wind. A young baby can feel a soft breeze on the skin, or maybe an adult will softly blow on the baby's body. A hairdryer can show how moving air can make other objects move, even though we can't see the air. Wind is moving air and is caused by differences in air pressure within our atmosphere. Air under high pressure moves towards areas of low pressure. The greater the difference in pressure, the faster the air flows. Another way of explaining this is that some parts of the earth are much warmer than others. The warm air produced by the sun rises and cooler air moves in underneath. It is this movement of air which makes the wind blow. A wind vane is used to measure the wind direction and an anemometer measures the wind speed.

The direction of the wind is expressed as the direction from which the wind is blowing. For example, easterly winds blow from east to west, while westerly winds blow from west to east. Winds have different levels of speed, such as 'breeze' and 'gale', depending on how fast they blow. Wind speeds are based on the descriptions of winds in a scale called the Beaufort scale, which divides wind speeds into 12 different categories, from less than 1mph to more than 73mph. If children become interested in this, there is good example of the Beaufort scale, using language children can understand, on the website: www.weatherwizkids.com.

Experiencing wind can be very different at different times of the year, depending on other weather conditions. Children need to have the freedom to experience wind for themselves. They may enjoy just running around with sheer exhilaration and excitement on a windy day. They may feel the wind blowing through their hair or onto their skin.

A raw winter wind coming from the north brings tears to our eyes and we all need to be well wrapped up and keep moving. This is in direct contrast to a cooling summer breeze, or a mad March wind in spring time.

It is important to be aware of the weather forecast. If there is a severe weather warning or a forecast of gales in your area, children should not be taken outside for their own safety.

Wind power

Some children may be familiar with wind farms. The large white turbines are powered by the wind to produce electricity. Old-fashioned windmills work in a slightly different way as their blades slow down the speed of the wind. The wind flows over the airfoil-shaped blades causing lift, like the effect on aeroplane wings, causing them to turn. The blades are connected to a drive shaft that turns an electric generator to produce electricity. Toy windmills are easily obtainable from garden centres. They are produced in a wide range of attractive colours and babies and toddlers will enjoy watching them.

Children may enjoy making their own windmills. Brightly coloured squares can be folded along a diagonal line into the middle and pinned with a mapping pin. Children will probably need help with this. It can then be pinned on to a stick. Paper sails can be added to model boats or attached to pieces of wood or bark. The boats will move freely over a builders' tray filled with water or a construction of waterways made from gutters and pipes.

Children will enjoy making their own kites or paper aeroplanes. Ribbon streamers can be attached to a fence and even very young children will enjoy watching the movement.

Wind direction

A simple test to find out the direction of the wind is to lick a finger and hold it up. The side of your finger that feels cold indicates where the wind is coming from. Windsocks are used in airports and children may enjoy making a simple windsock out of an old sock with the end cut out or by making one from a strip of fabric. Cutting out streamers and ribbons and tying them to a fence or onto a stick or tree may also appeal.

Look out for:

- Objects blown around by the wind (small objects can be collected on a windy day by hanging up paper plates smeared with petroleum jelly).
- Plants that use the wind to help disperse seeds such as dandelions, thistles, hawkweeds and willow herb.
- Sycamore seeds (helicopters) – throw them up and watch them swirling and twirling down again.
- Leaves blowing around on the ground or down from the trees in autumn.
- Cloud patterns in the sky.

Talk about:

- Wind chimes in your outdoor space (young babies will hear the sounds and toddlers may enjoy experimenting with chimes at a lower level).
- Bells of different sizes may also be hung for children to strike or for the wind to blow.
- Tall grasses in beds or even a few in a flowerpot will give babies something to watch as they move around in the light and also provide a soft, rustling sound on a breezy day.
- A selection of streamers for younger children to watch and older children to use to twirl and dance – they may move like trees in the wind or leaves blowing around; try making up simple verses about the wind using different sound words such as whooo, whoosh, swish, rustle etc.
- Materials to make a shelter from the wind – blankets over an A-frame, or a pop-up tent (decide which way the wind is blowing and which would be the best place for the entrance).
- Bubble mixture, large bubble blowers and bats – good for very windy days (look at the colours and reflections of light in the bubbles and consider how far the bubbles travel).
- Straws and watery paint show how air currents can move paint, and children may want to experiment with paint and water on a windy day.

Children can blow large bubbles with special blowers and watch the reflections of light as the bubbles blow away in the wind.

A windy day box

Assemble a collection of:
- string
- cord
- bulldog clips
- lengths of ribbon and fabric
- light fabrics such as gauze and chiffon
- coloured spinners
- wind chimes
- toy windmills (garden centres now stock these if you are not near a beach shop)
- soft hair bands and wristbands
- paper and card
- wooden sticks
- glue and sticky tape
- grill shelf to which to attach streamers if you have no fence

- mini kites
- natural resources such as sycamore seeds, leaves and dandelion heads
- some of the storybooks listed in further resources below
- flags and bunting
- bubble mix (or washing-up liquid) and blowers
- straws
- paint.

Further resources

Stories

Mrs Mopple's Washing Line by Anita Hewitt (Red Fox 2004).
The Wind Blew by Pat Hutchins (Atheneum Books 1993).
The Windy Day by Anna Milbourne (Usborne Books 2012).
Feel the Wind (Let's Read and Find Out Science) by Arthur Dorros (William Morrow 2001).
Walters's Windy Washing Line by Neil Griffiths (Red Robin Books 2001).
www.weatherwizkids.com
An excellent source of reference and moving icons, which will appeal to children if they wish to look at this site with an adult.

Art

A Windy Day by David Cox.
Shows an old-fashioned windmill.

Summer Wind by Vladimir Volakov.
The Gust of Wind by Jean Baptists-Camille Corot.
The March Wind by Lisa Berkshire.
Windy Day by Gerald Stokes.
A painting showing a family of teddy bears out for a walk and one being lifted up by an umbrella and flying in the wind.

Windy Day in Auxerre by Chaim Soutine (1939).
The above pictures can be found at www.worldgallery.co.uk.

Windmills near Zaandam by Claude Monet.
This picture can be found at www.claudemonetgallery.org.

Various photographs of wind turbines can be found on the internet.

Fog and mist

It is difficult to know where to place fog and mist as it is a natural combination of the two elements of air and water. Depending where you live, some children may experience fog and mist on a fairly regular basis, but for some it may be something that happens only very occasionally and may provoke children's curiosity and questions. The difference between fog and mist is only the density of the tiny droplets of water that cause it. Fog can be the result of different weather conditions, but always involves very moist and relatively cold air that doesn't rise. It is the result of air being cooled to the point (actually, the dew point temperature) where it can no longer hold all of the water vapour it contains. As the air can no longer hold its moisture it is turned into droplets and that is when fog appears. It can be thought of as a cloud at ground level.

Sea mist can hang low over coastal towns, creating a cold, damp environment at the same time that inland towns have hot sunshine. This is caused by an overload of moisture in the air over the sea, which drifts inland and often hangs there for much of the day.

Look out for:

- Outlines of trees and buildings.
- Shapes of branches in the mist.
- Droplets of moisture caught on spiders' webs and on plants.
- Blurred shapes in the distance.

Talk about:

- Why you can't see very far – use words such as visibility, blurred, distant, misty, moist etc.
- What you can hear – do sounds sound the same as when it is clear?
- The use of sound in fog – as a warning, e.g. foghorns on ships and lighthouses, hooters on bikes.
- Sound as a means of location, e.g. whistles on misty mountains.
- The use of lights as warnings, e.g. lighthouse, fog lights on cars, torches to find our way.
- Reflective lights.

A foggy day box

Assemble a collection of:

- torches
- reflective arm bands
- other items of reflective clothing
- fabrics, string and pegs to make cosy dens
- sound instruments, cones, beaters, drums (can be made from all sorts of containers)
- flexible hose, fog horns, bicycle bells and horns
- mirrors to collect water droplets
- whistles
- bicycle bells
- musical instruments that can be used to guide children when they cannot see
- glow sticks
- a camera
- tubes
- cans for telephone
- ropes and quoits for trails
- lighthouse
- boats
- tracing paper.

Further resources

Stories

The Foggy Foggy Forest by Mick Sharratt (Walker 2008).
Postman Pat's Foggy Day by John Cunnliffe (Scholastic 1983).

Art

Waterloo Bridge by Claude Monet.
Oak Grove in Fog by William Guion.
Autumn Mist Poster by Donna Geissler.
Trees in Fog by Chris Honeysett.
All the above and more can be found at www.allposters.co.uk.

Conclusion

It is easy to take for granted that air is present all around us at all times, and children will gradually develop an understanding of this concept. Wind is usually the first time they become aware of air and we need to encourage curiosity and questioning. Exercise can also be used to help them understand the nature of breathing and our dependence on air for survival. Mist and fog are weather conditions that link air and water and help us to see something of the delicate balance of the elements as they both combine and separate, affecting each other and creating the world in which we live.

11 | Water

Playing with water is something that comes naturally to young children and most settings provide some experiences which allow children to interact with water. The quality of the experience may be defined by space and convenience, but where children are given a range of high quality experiences on a daily basis they will benefit in many ways. They will develop fine motor control, an understanding of mathematical properties of volume and weight, as well as improved cooperation, strategic thinking, sociability and imagination.

A childminder can arrange for a child to stand at the sink ,or place a washing-up bowl and plastic-covered surface at the child's level.

Water can be provided in individual trays (cat litter trays are a good size) with mini funnels and small plastic bottles and containers. These trays are also good for making bubbles, foam or mixing water with other substances such as cornflour or compost.

Many settings offer a larger water tray, but it needs to be well resourced. Children should be able to access a range of funnels, jugs, pipes and bottles. Younger children may need a smaller selection as they may take everything and fill up the tray. Protective clothing should be easy to put on and take off, although again, younger children will need some help with this.

Supplied occasionally, fishing nets, small boats, plastic fish and sea-life creatures can add variety to the play and will stimulate language.

Water play outdoors may mean children can experiment more freely as it doesn't matter if water is spilt. Providing a very deep water container such as a zinc bath, together with some larger jugs and plastic containers, will give children an opportunity to explore weight and volume. Pipes and gutters will allow children to develop concepts of gradients, siphoning and movement of water. Duct tape can be used if necessary to fix these in place.

Rain

There was a time when nursery staff used to dread wet days as it meant that children remained inside for most of the day, with the consequent restlessness and challenges of keeping them all interested and involved. As we have got more and more used to being outside with our children, it becomes even more difficult to stay in. Therefore, we need to consider how we can actively involve children outdoors on wet days. It may be that staff members are somewhat more resistant to being outside and some may really dislike getting wet. One of the first resources, therefore, needs to be some wet weather gear!

Younger children may wear all-in-one suits, but as they get older and are able to dress themselves, it is wiser to buy separate rain tops and rain trousers. Wellies are essential items and parents can usually supply these, but it is a good idea to have some spares. Jumble sales and car boot sales are a good source of wellies. Adults, too, need to have wellies, as well as a waterproof top and, for very wet days, a pair of waterproof trousers.

Well organised storage and space near the door will encourage children to dress themselves before they go out and similarly undress on return. A large door mat may help with problems of mud and wet, and children should learn to wipe their feet or take off their wellies in a porch if there is one.

Going out in the rain with young children can be enormous fun, especially when there are puddles around. Some children may not have experienced being outside in the rain as they are usually protected by plastic covers on the buggy or are inside a car. Just going for a wet walk can be a new and exciting experience as they feel the rain on their hands and cheeks, or stick out their tongue to catch raindrops.

Rain comes in many different forms. Cold winter rain that blows horizontally in a gale will lash our cheeks and it may be that a short walk is enough. Children will be able to experience a healthy glow as they return inside to get warm and dry. Soft spring rain is easier to be out in for longer periods of time. Children can experience rain drops and hear them falling on the roof of a den or nearby leaves. A sudden spring or summer shower may just as suddenly stop and, when the sun comes out, there is a magical quality as raindrops glisten on leaves and grass. Children love to use umbrellas in their play (make sure that they understand the need to use them safely) and will shelter under them. A piece of aluminium foil on top of the umbrella enhances the sounds of the raindrops.

Look out for:

- Suitable places to go in the rain, particularly if you have no outdoor space of your own.
- Somewhere where you can create your own puddles if you have a level outdoor surface.

Talk about:

- Cloud colours and patterns in the sky.
- How we know if it's going to rain.
- Why we need to dress up before going out in the rain, what is special about our rain clothes and how they are different.
- The sounds raindrops make on different surfaces (heavy rain is very different from a shower).
- The taste of raindrops on the tongue.

Supply:

- Spare wellies, raincoats and trousers for children and staff (many websites now offer these at reasonable prices).
- Umbrellas of different sizes – put foil on top of some as this makes a different sound.
- A range of containers of different shapes to collect rainwater.
- Measuring cylinders.

(Also see detailed list of resources at the end of this section.)

Dens in the rain

Dens need to be available at all times, but there is something particularly attractive about sheltering from the rain in a den you have made yourself. Pop-up tents can be used or supply a tarpaulin or plastic sheet and drape it over a rope attached to two poles or between two trees.

Puddle play

The appeal of puddles is rather like walking through autumn leaves. It seems to stretch beyond childhood. Observation has shown that if adults are wearing wellies, they will walk through a puddle rather than go round it. Similarly, children will want to walk through a puddle, regardless of what they have on their feet. There is something innately fascinating about this experience as we reconnect with the rain and the mud. From a very early age babies and toddlers love to explore puddles. It is important therefore that we are able to offer this experience to all the children in our care. Out on a walk there is a sense of adventure and risk-taking as children step into a large puddle and wonder whether the water will come over their wellies. Similarly, if it is very muddy there is a sense of fear as the wellies stick in the mud and it becomes more difficult to wade out. Sometimes they even lose a wellie in the process.

Children will use a range of materials if they are allowed to play in puddles. They will explore floating and sinking, transporting water from one puddle to another, and using a stick or throwing in a pebble, which is a start to learning about ripples and the movements of water.

Water play

Water play is a way of involving children from a very early age in exploratory play. They become deeply involved and will experiment with water in a range of ways. Very young babies like to stretch out their hands to splash. By using the rain as a natural resource and thinking about it as an extension of water play, you will be able to extend these experiences for children of all ages. There was a time when we used to provide a tray half-full of warm water and felt we had provided sufficiently for water exploration. Now we are more adventurous in our thinking and through observing very young children and their fascination with natural resources we can provide richer experiences in our settings.

Builders' trays on the ground will collect rainwater and children can use the natural materials available to experiment with floating and sinking. I still do not understand though why some conkers sink and some float!

Exploring water after rain will help children in their understanding of the natural environment and the changes within it.

Look at the resource lists at the end of the chapter and think about how children can use these resources. Pipes and gutters can be taped onto vertical surfaces such as fences or seats. Alternatively, you could use bricks to prop them up to make a waterway. Children can float small boats down these using watering cans or jugs to aid the flow.

Children can use large containers to transport water around, and there is less need to worry about spillages if they are already wearing their rain clothes.

Making potions

There is something magical about making potions and mixes. Children love to collect a wide range of natural materials and mix them together. By using rainwater that has been collected, children will be using another natural resource and also learning something about conserving our tap water supply. As children get older, the concoctions become more imaginative and, through discussion with adults, children will invent more scenarios and may be able to begin to write down a recipe for the 'brew'.

Children talk together as they look at their reflections in the puddle.

Mark-making in the rain

Puddles appeal to children from a very young age. Babies will crawl towards them and going for wet walk with a toddler often doesn't go much further than the first few puddles. Children become transfixed by jumping and splashing. A nearby twig or stick will encourage children to make marks in the puddle and surrounding mud.

Coloured paint can be added to rain water and children can use it to make patterns in shallow trays or on the ground. Wet paper offers a different texture and painting in the rain will be very different from painting inside. Spray bottles with paint can be used on paper out in the rain. The rain will mix with the colours to great effect. Different sizes of paint brushes and rollers can be used.

Puddles can be marked by chalk and as they dry out, older children will be able to observe the process of evaporation and maybe record the size of the puddle at regular intervals.

Riding bicycles in the rain is great fun and children can make tracks and splashes as they ride through puddles. If it has stopped raining and there is some dry ground, they can see how far the tyre marks will go.

Water conservation

As I write this, we are having an official drought but it has rained solidly for the last few days and so much water is going to waste. Children need to learn about conservation and understand what a precious resource we have in our fresh water. Water barrels can be supplied for children to help themselves to water for watering plants and mixing in with soil to make mud. Watering flowers and vegetables is necessary when the ground is dry and children will learn that water is a vital ingredient for plants to thrive.

Rainbows

Spotting a rainbow can be very exciting and children will enjoy looking at the colours of the rainbow. The order in which they appear is red, orange, yellow, green, blue, indigo and violet. Rainbows are formed when the sun shines from a low position through drops of moisture in the atmosphere. If the rainbow is seen against a darkened sky it is easier to pick out the colours.

Children love to draw or paint rainbows and it is important to ensure that they have a supply of red, orange, yellow, green, blue, indigo and violet materials. (Indigo is a shade of bluey-purple, which lies between blue and violet.)

Creative experiences

After listening to the rain, children may be able to recreate the sound of raindrops with musical instruments. Rain sticks can be bought or children can make their own by putting some rice or dried peas in a tube, sealing it well at both ends and decorating as they wish.

Large plastic containers can be used as drums for children to drum out the rhythms of the raindrops. A range of metallic instruments can also be suspended for children to make patterns based on the rhythm of the rain. However, if you have a good range of natural materials, children will be able to create different sounds using sticks, stones and pieces of wood of different lengths and thicknesses.

In one setting, when it suddenly started to rain in the summer, two girls rushed out in the rain just wearing their summer dresses and started to dance spontaneously. Staff did not interrupt this as they were having such a wonderful time and at the end, just calmly gave them a dry set of clothes.

'Winter' from *The Four Seasons* by Vivaldi is a good piece of music to listen to the sound of slow raindrops.

Further resources

A rainy day bin

This bin could contain:

- short lengths of hosepipe, plastic piping and short lengths of household guttering

- down pipes and connectors
- watering cans, umbrellas, paint droppers and squeezy bottles of different sizes
- a roll of strong waterproof tape (duct tape is ideal).

A rainy day box

Assemble a collection of:
- a selection of containers to catch the rain
- small funnels, jugs and bottles
- a selection of large and small spoons for mixing, pouring and stirring
- a colander or sieve
- washing-up liquid and food colouring or paints
- small plastic animals, fish and cartons to make boats
- an unbreakable mirror to catch raindrops
- magnifiers
- plastic sheeting or tarpaulin
- a selection of fabrics to test water resistance, e.g. cotton, gauze, wool, plastic, chamois, denim and polyester.

Rhymes

I hear thunder
It's raining, it's pouring
Rain, rain, go away
Incey wincey spider

Stories

Kipper's Rainy Day by Mick Inkpen (Hodder Children's Books 2001).
Rainy Day: Get Dressed for Splishy Splashy Fun by Caroline Church (Barrons Educational Services 2009).
Mrs. Wishy Washy's Splishy Splashy Day by Joy Cowley (Shortland 2001).
Where Do They Go When it Rains? By Gerda Muller (Floris 2010).
The Rainy Day by Anna Milbourne (Usborne 2012).

Totally absorbed in her play, this child has used paints in the rain and built her own shelter.

Thunderstorms

Thunderstorms can occur at any time of year, but they are particularly common if the weather has been excessively hot and humid. They often occur in the afternoon or evening.

Children can be frightened of thunder and lightning and may need a lot or reassurance during a storm. Young children do not like the sudden loud noises and the flashes of lightning are very bright. Often it is possible to see the dark purple cumulonimbus clouds advancing and hear the thunder from a distance. Adults need to be reassuring and explain that this is a result of warm, moist air rising up and forming electricity. Lightning flashes are a result of this and as they leave the cloud, they make an air pocket which then collapses causing the sound effect we know as thunder.

Children also need to learn that it is dangerous to be outside in a thunderstorm and that even indoors there are certain precautions that need to be taken. Computers and televisions should be switched off in case of a lightning strike. Also, it is better to avoid contact with water during a storm, as the water can act as a lightning conductor.

Some children may be curious as to what makes the thunder and lightning. Lightning is a bright flash of electricity produced by a thunderstorm. In a thundercloud, many small bits of ice (frozen raindrops) bump into each other as they move around in the air. All of those collisions create an electric charge. After a while, the whole cloud fills up with electrical charges. The positive charges, or protons, form at the top of the cloud and the negative charges, or electrons, form at the bottom of the cloud. Since opposites attract, that causes a positive charge to build up on the ground beneath the cloud. The electrical charge on the ground concentrates around anything that sticks up, such as mountains, people or single trees. The charge coming up from these points eventually connects with a charge reaching down from the clouds and – zap – lightning strikes!

Thunder is actually caused by lightning. When a lightning bolt travels from the cloud to the ground, it actually opens up a little hole in the air called a channel. Once the light is gone, the air collapses back in and creates the sound wave that we hear as thunder. The reason we see lightning before we hear thunder, is because light travels faster than sound.

Children can enjoy counting the number of seconds that elapse between the lightning flash and the next thunder rumble. This gives us an estimate of how far away the storm is. The number of seconds counted needs to be divided by five. Every five seconds represents one mile. If you count to ten, the storm would be approximately two miles away.

Using musical instruments and torches, children can re-enact the storm and this is often something that can help to allay any fears they may have. 'I hear thunder' is often sung and children can use rainsticks or shakers to imitate the sound of the rain. Try to use words to describe it such as bang, crash, flash, rumble, grumble etc. Children may be able to make up a rhyme using these words.

A good story to use on this theme is *After the storm – Percy's Park* by Nick Butterworth (Harper Collins 2001).

Hail

Hail is a strange weather phenomenon as it can occur at all times of the year; even in the summer small balls of ice can lie on the ground. It is not a weather condition that children should be outside in, but they will be fascinated by listening to the sound on a metal or glass roof, or watching it through a window.

Hail is formed in huge cumulonimbus clouds, commonly known as thunderheads. When the ground is heated during the day by the sun, the air close to the ground is heated as well. Hot air, being less dense and therefore lighter than cold air, rises and cools. As the rising air cools, its capacity for holding moisture decreases. When the rising warm air has cooled so much that it cannot retain all of its moisture, water vapour condenses, forming puffy-looking clouds. The condensing moisture releases heat of its own into the surrounding air, causing the air to rise faster and give up even more moisture. There are strong updrafts in the cloud and often the cloud will contain frozen raindrops, dust or salt. If the temperature is below zero, the water vapour freezes on to these particles forming hailstones. If they make contact with super cooled water on their descent they will become larger and heavier. Once they become too heavy for the strong upward current to support them, they fall from the sky. In a matter of moments, the ground can be covered in hailstones, transforming it into a white icy sheet. If you think it might hail, place a variety of containers large and small outside. When the storm has stopped, children will be able to go out and collect the ice. Using magnifying glasses they can examine the hailstones and watch them melt as they remain in the warmer temperatures at ground level.

In some countries, hail storms occur frequently and the hail stones are big enough to cause damage to crops and even buildings. Older children might be interested to know that the largest hailstone ever documented weighed 0.75 kilograms (1.67 pounds), and spanned 14.4 centimetres (5.67 inches). It fell in Kansas in 1970.

Snow

Adults may have mixed feelings when snow is forecast. We remember the difficulties of trying to get to work, do the shopping, and the need to be careful whenever we go out. Children, on the other hand, are usually excited and cannot wait to get outside. Parents and staff alike need to ensure that they and the children are well wrapped up before venturing outside. Warm clothing is essential and several thin layers are a better way of keeping warm. Make sure that parents know that children will be going out and are dressed appropriately. Keep a box of spare clothing so all children can go out if they wish. Spare wellies and waterproof gloves are a must.

There is something magical about watching the feathery flakes of snow as they float and whirl down from a leaden sky. A heavy fall of snow can transform the outdoor space within a very short time and there will be lots of conversations as children watch the snow falling.

Weather forecasts have been somewhat more reliable recently, but we are still not always well prepared for snow. In your setting, it is useful to have certain resources readily available, so children can maximise the opportunities to be outside and enjoy the experience of snow.

Babies can go out if they are wearing warm snowsuits but they need to be checked frequently to see they don't get cold. Hands and feet are often vulnerable. Toddlers may be unsure if this is the first time they have walked on snow, and they may prefer to sit on a sledge or just sit down in the snow. They need the constant presence of a reassuring adult and may not wish to handle the snow at all. Some toddlers, on the other hand, are fearless and enjoy being pulled along on a sledge or even sledging down a hill.

Encourage children to make different things out of snow. It doesn't always need to be a snowman. Try snow birds, fish, a dinosaur or a castle. Natural materials can be used to decorate their creations. Even a light snowfall will provide enough for a mini snowperson or a fantasy creature.

If you have some old cake tins, children can make snow pies and even put bread crumbs on top to leave out for the birds.

Snow provides good opportunities for mark making. Encourage children to look out for footprints, but also to look closely at their own. Small rakes and sticks or twigs will be good for children to make patterns and marks. Take photographs of tracks in the snow and discuss with the children what or who might have passed that way.

Collecting snow and placing it inside on a builders' trays will encourage children to play in different ways and also make observations on the different speeds of melting compared to the snow outside.

Children may wish to use instruments and make up a snowflakes dance. They will be able to draw and make books from their own experiences outside. Tasting snowflakes and icicles is all part of the fun.

Look out for:

- Ice forming on ponds, water trays and buckets of water outside.
- Icicles hanging from buildings.
- Footprints in the snow, the different sizes of human prints, animal and bird tracks, and the tracks of bikes and toys.
- Patterns of snowflakes, using a magnifying glass.
- Snow melting outside, and also inside if you take any indoors.
- Birds searching for food.

Talk about:

- The need to keep warm and to wear suitable clothes.

- Why we have ice and snow in the winter (use a thermometer to record outside temperatures and use the words 'degrees' and 'minus'; older children may be able to understand the fact that we don't have snow in the summer as the earth is nearer the sun – we sometimes have snow in late autumn or early spring).

- Making a simple graph to show temperatures – the higher the number, the colder the air (explain the meaning of minus).

- Why ice is slippery.

- Why we need to feed the birds.

- The crystal shapes of snowflakes – what causes snow.

- Snow hanging on trees and shrubs.

- Snow glistening and sparkling when the sun comes out.

- Snowflakes, blizzards (usually occur if it's windy), a flurry of snow or a hailstorm.

- What makes the snow thaw.

- Countries where they have much more snow than we do – look at a globe and discuss the polar regions, the Arctic and the Antarctic.

- Which animals live in these countries, why polar bears are white, and how these animals survive.

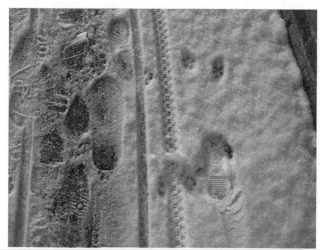

Taking a photograph or observing tracks in the snow first hand will encourage children to discuss and think imaginatively about who or what might have passed their way.

Supply:

- Spare clothing
  - — spare wellies, even if children have their own.
  - — spare gloves and woolly hats so children can change if theirs get wet.
  - — some all-in-one suits for children who may not have suitable outer clothes.
- Small bean bags on radiators to warm chilly hands when children come back in.
- Buckets, spades and rakes – useful tools for building a snowman.
- Twigs, cones and stones for snowmen or simply to make marks and patterns in the snow.
- Small wheelbarrows to move snow around.
- Large plastic trays to hold snow to take inside so children can observe melting.
- Lenses and magnifying glasses.
- A good supply of white paint and white crayons.
- Thick and thin brushes available for children to select.
- Dark paper – grey or black.
- Chalks of different colours, charcoal and pastels.
- White fabrics and tissue for collage.
- A fully charged digital camera (encourage children to look closely at the way the snow sits on the trees and take some close-up pictures; this can be used as part of a display and maybe children can talk and make up poems about the pictures).

Further resources

Stories

Elmer in the Snow by David McKee (Andersen Press 2008).

Tiger in the Snow by Nick Butterworth (Harper Collins Children's Books 2008).

One Snowy Night – A Tale from Percy's Park by Nick Butterworth (Harper Collins Children's Books 2001).

Foxes in the Snow by J. Emnett (Macmillan Children's Books 2008).

A beautifully illustrated story about two mischievous fox cubs exploring snow for the first time.

The Snowy Day by Anna Milbourne (Usborne Books 2005).
A Bird in Winter – A Children's Book Inspired by Peter Breughel by H. Kerrillis (Prostel 2011).
Children can learn about Breughel and his art as they enter a world of snow and the beauty of a winter's day (based on the picture 'Hunter in the snow' by Breughel).

The Snowman by Raymond Briggs (Penguin 2002).
Also music by Howard Blake. CD and story book also available on video.

Art

Art poster from www.allposters.com:

The Magpie by Claude Monet.
This shows winter light on snow in the country.

Poems

'The more it snows tiddly pom' from *Winnie the Pooh* by A. A. Milne, in *The Complete Tales and Poems of Winnle the Pooh* (Egmont 2001).

Conclusion

Water is probably one of the most diverse play resources available. However, we are now much more aware of the importance of water conservation and this awareness is something we need to highlight to children. Using rain and puddles on a rainy day is a natural way of making the most of this as a play resource. When designing our outdoor spaces, it is important to include ways to collect rainwater for both play purposes and gardening. Children can use small bottles or watering cans to help themselves, but adults must stress the importance of not drinking rainwater and ensure that there is always a supply of drinking water that children can access easily. If a water tray is filled indoors from a tap it is sometimes possible to empty this into containers to use for watering plants, particularly in dry periods.

Snow and ice present us with challenges and opportunities. We need to encourage children to enjoy these experiences, but also to be aware of problems and possible dangers that can arise. If children are able to experience snow first-hand, they will be able to understand more easily the climates and habitats of other parts of our world.

12 | Fire

Ever since man discovered fire and how he could make and control it, it has been used to meet our basic needs. Young children growing up in a cave would have lived closely with fire as it was used to heat their home and cook their food. It also offered protection from danger as it warned off wild animals.

Many young children are fascinated by fire and there seems to be something of this basic instinct left in many of us. However, there is currently such a strong climate of protection and safety that many children are not exposed to fire, and consequently never really learn how to behave safely and act responsibly when near it.

Lighting a campfire and cooking on it is now an integral part of a forest school session. It is conducted when children have already had some days when their awareness of their natural surroundings has been increased and they have learned to listen and respond appropriately to rules. Children know that they are not allowed to walk across the space in front of the fire. They learn to sit safely for several sessions in the space with an unlit fire. When it is time to light the fire, an adult is always present and children are able to sit safely, watch the wispy smoke as the fire begins to take hold, the orange flames licking around the wood, and hear the crackling of wood as it burns. They feel the heat as it grows stronger. They smell the smoke and taste the food or drink that has been prepared out in the open. They learn that matches are only to be used by an adult and that fire needs to be treated with respect.

Many practitioners and parents are still wary of children being close to an open fire. However, the benefits are so great that I would recommend the practice. It is an essential part of the experience of growing up with respect for outdoor spaces. Knowledge of fire and the damage it can cause to our natural environment needs to be instilled in everyone. Safe use of fire could save lives and protect our wildlife habitat.

Practitioners who are cautious about this will benefit from some training sessions and the opportunity to voice their concerns. Risk assessments will be conducted and it may mean a change of policy for some settings. Any fire needs to be lit in a designated space or fire pit. In forest school, children sit on logs with no physical barrier between them and the fire. However this happens over time, as explained above, and adults need to be constantly aware, particularly if there are children who may need additional supervision. This is also dependent on using a permanent space where the fire area is in a fire pit and can be located at least three metres away from nearby walls, fencing, overhanging branches or buildings.

In a smaller outdoor space, it may be possible to use a flowerbed or digging area at the end of the growing season. Alternatively, consider using a fire bowl, now easily obtainable from garden centres or online, or use a ready-prepared barbecue so children can toast marshmallows or bananas. This needs to be placed safely on soil, sand or a safe hard surface. Invest, too, in a pair of fireproof gloves. They can be used when cooking but are also useful when lighting and extinguishing the fire.

If necessary, children can remain behind a safety barrier made of crates. They will still experience the smell of the smoke and the sight and sound of the flames. They will still learn about the safe use of matches and the need for an adult to have control.

Once practitioners are confident, parents need to be informed of the reasons for this activity and also the safety precautions that are in place. At Nutfield Nursery children are given initial training about how to behave around a fire and parents are also offered fire training. They can then see the benefits to their children and know they are safe to be around fire. When the clocks go back, the children often end their day around the fire in the dusk and parents collect them from there to go home.

Cooking vegetables in a soup over the fire or just boiling water for a hot drink is a wonderful experience for children. Children in one nursery make bonfire soup, using ingredients that resemble the colour of flames (see recipe in Appendix).

After the fire has been extinguished, the children can use the charred wood to make charcoal and use it for drawing.

Talk about:

- The colours and shapes of the flame.
- Wisps of smoke curling upwards.
- Why there is sometimes more smoke than flame.
- What is needed to make the flames.
- The sounds you can hear, such as the crackle of twigs.
- The smell of the smoke and what happens if it gets in your eyes.
- The need to obey the rules and possible consequences.
- The safe use of matches.
- How fire was used for light, heat and cooking for many centuries before the invention of electricity.

A permanent fire space can be created if there is enough room and children learn how to behave safely. They can then experience the smell of the smoke and the sound of crackling twigs.

Further resources

Forest Schools and Outdoor Learning in the Early Years by Sara Knight (Sage Publications 2009).

www.ltl.org.uk

March 2012 Profiles Article – 'FAQ: What do I need to consider before installing a fire pit?'

www.historyforkids.org/learn/science/fire.htm

Children may develop their imaginary play around fire engines and firefighters and you may need to provide play resources such as helmets, hosepipes and mobile phones, or alternatively encourage them to use natural resources for these.

Conclusion

Fire is elemental and holds a strange fascination for all of us. Some children seem to be particularly attracted to fire. Having opportunities at a young age to experience safe fire could go a long way to lessen the risk of experimenting without supervision. Sitting around a campfire is a very special experience and creates feelings of security and fellowship as well as offering a deep sensory experience. Cooking and eating around a fire adds another dimension and links us to our ancestors, creating a sense of timelessness and slowing down the frenetic pace at which we live. Like all the elements it reconnects us to our roots and gives us a sense of belonging in our world. It also deepens our understanding and hopefully our desire to live our lives with respect for the elements and the part they play.

Further resources about weather and the elements

The Little Book of Outside in All Weathers by S. Featherstone (A&C Black 2011).
The Little Book of Sand and Water by S. Featherstone (A&C Black 2011).
Playing and Learning Outdoors by Jan White (Routledge 2008).
The Big Alfie Out of Doors Story Book by Shirley Hughes (Red Fox 1994).
Alfie's Weather by Shirley Hughes (Red Fox 2002).
Planning for Learning Through the Weather by Rachel Sparks Linfield (Step Forward Publishing 2008).
Maisy's Wonderful Weather Book by Lucy Cousins (Walker 2007).
How the Weather Works by Christiane Donan and Beverley Young (Templar 2011).
My Best Book of Weather by Simon Adams (Kingfisher 2008).
Elmer's Weather by David Mckee (Andersen Press 1994).
Weather – 200 Facts by Clare Oliver (Miles Kelly Publishing 2006).
A good reference book of facts for children and adults to share together.

www.weatherwizkids.com
A useful source of facts about weather and what causes weather changes.

Conclusion

The weather and the seasons have a direct influence on our daily lives – more than we probably realise. Even for those of us who do not spend much time interacting with the natural world, our habits are governed by the time of year and the weather. We dress according to the weather, and how we spend our leisure time is often dictated by the time of year as well as the weather.

Musicians, artists, poets and sculptors are inspired by the natural world around them. Familiar poetic lines about dancing daffodils or season of mists and mellow fruitfulness are the result of the intimate relationship between adults and nature. If we ourselves have been able to develop this relationship, it is more likely that we are able to maintain our own creative and emotional well-being.

From an early age, children are naturally drawn to the outdoors and the plants and animals that live there. However, it is evident that many are not given the opportunity to interact with this world on a daily basis, spending much of their time indoors and, as they get older, more and more time in front of a screen. Research highlights the need to offer children alternative experiences. Tim Gill (2007) writes that:

> Climbing a tree, working out how to start testing for strength, feeling how the breeze in your face also sways the branches underfoot, glimpsing the changing vista through the leaves, dreaming about being king or queen of the jungles, shouting to your friends below, once you've got as high as you dare – is an immersive 360-degree experience that virtual or indoor settings simply cannot compare with.
>
> (Quoted in Moss 2012: 5)

This book has suggested a range of outdoor experiences and offered ideas to create outdoor spaces or find ways of taking children to wider spaces. It embodies the pedagogy of play, and suggests that there are two main aspects in the role of the practitioner. Pedagogical framing, as outlined by Iram Siraj-Blatchford *et al.* in the

REPEY report (2002), involves the planning and resourcing of the outdoor learning space. The pedagogical interaction comes in the way adults involve children and share with them in a wider range of outdoor experiences.

The practitioner's role is therefore proactive, both in creating the environment and also responding to children's interests and promoting the characteristics of effective learning. Creating an environment that is as natural as possible will offer places to hide and places to explore. It will be dynamic and vary from day to day and season to season.

An awareness of the beauty around us will help us to stop for a moment with the children to look at cloud patterns in the sky, or the dewdrops on a spider's web. We need to be able to answer the questions, 'How did the spider make the web? Is it really going to eat the fly?'

We will offer our children cognitive experiences as they observe life cycles and grow flowers and vegetables. We will also be exposing them to a range of emotional experiences. They will learn about winners and losers in the animal world, they will experience fear and danger. They will learn about birth and death, growth and decay. They may become cold or wet or even get hurt, but these difficult experiences serve to prepare them for the challenges of the adult world. Above all, they will develop a sense of respect and an appreciation of natural beauty.

Ofsted recognises that:

> Outdoor learning gives children direct experience making it more interesting and enhancing their understanding. Children who learn outdoors, know more, understand more, feel better, behave better, work more cooperatively and are physically healthier. This is not just for able or more motivated pupils: underachievers also do better in a natural environment, especially when exposed to high quality stimulating activities.
>
> (Ofsted 2008 cited in Moss 2012: 9)

If we can encourage children to become interested in the natural world from an early age, they will have a better chance of being able to access it for themselves in later life. They will also be aware of the need to conserve and care for our natural resources. Many research studies that indicate that children benefit from everyday experience with the natural environment also recognise the implications for the future of our world. In a report from the United Nations Convention on Biological Diversity, Dr. Ahmed Djoghal writes:

> Children's knowledge of biodiversity is in decline at a time when we need future generations to be more engaged and aware in order to halt its loss. There is a very real need to educate our children as future guardians of our planet, to provide them with the knowledge they need today to preserve the natural world tomorrow.
>
> (Quoted in RSPB 2010: 8)

David Attenborough said in a conference speech (Communicate 2010) that 'No one will protect what they don't care about and no one will care about what they have never experienced'.

So go outside every day, come wind, rain, hail or shine. Take your pupils, your children and your grandchildren with you. Find something to look at, to talk about, to share and to enjoy. This sharing of experience is fundamental to all learning.

Bibliography

Bird, W. (2007) *Natural Thinking: Investigating the Links Between the Natural Environment, Biodiversity and Mental Health*. Sandy, Bedfordshire: RSPB.

Carson, R. (1956) *The Sense of Wonder*. New York: Harper and Row.

Community Playthings (2007) *Lighting the Fire: Hands-on Investigation, Play and Outdoor Learning in Primary Education*. Available at: www.communityplaythings. co.uk/learning-library/training-resources/lighting-the-fire

Faber Taylor, A., Kuo, F. and Sullivan, W. (2001) 'Coping with ADD: The Surprising Connection to Green Play Settings', *Environment and Behaviour*, 33 (Jan 2001): 54–77.

Gibson, J. (1986) *The Ecological Approach to Visual Perception*. London: Psychology Press.

Gill, T. (2007) *No Fear: Growing up in a Risk Averse Society*. London: Caloust Gulbenkian Foundation.

Knight, S. (2009) *Forest Schools and Outdoor Learning in the Early Years*. London: Sage Publications.

Laevers, F., Daems, M., De Bruckyere, G., Declerq, B., Moons, J., Silkens, K., Snoeck, G. and Van Kesse, M. (2005) *Well being and Involvement in Care: A Process Oriented Self Evaluation Instrument for Care Settings*. Leuven, Belgium: Leuven University. Available online at www.kindengezin.be/img/sics-ziko-manual.pdf

Learning and Teaching Scotland (2010) *Curriculum for Excellence Through Outdoor Learning*. Obtainable from Learning and Teaching Scotland, The Optima, 58 Newton Street, Glasgow G2 8DU.

Lester, S. and Maudsley, M. (2006) *Play Naturally: A Review of Children's Natural Play*, commissioned by the Children's Play Council. Obtainable from National

Children's Bureau, c/o Central Books, 99 Wallis Road, London E9 5LN, or available online at www.playday.org.uk/PDF/play-naturally-a-review-of-childrens-natural%20play.pdf

London Sustainable Development Commission (2011) *Sowing the Seeds: Reconnecting London's Children with Nature – Executive Summary*. London: Greater London Authority.

Louv, R. (2005) *Last Child in the Woods: Saving our Children from Nature-Deficit Disorder*. London: Atlantic Books

Malone, K. and Tranter, P. (2003) 'Children's Environmental Learning and the Use, Design and Management of School Grounds', *Children, Youth and Environments*, 13(2): 283–303.

McMillan, M. (1919) *The Nursery School*. London: Dent.

Moore, R. (1997) 'The Need for Nature: A Childhood Right', *Social Justice*, 24(3): 203–13.

Moore, R. and Wong, H. (1997) *Natural Learning in Creating Environments for Rediscovering Nature's way of Teaching*. Berkley: MIG Communications.

Moss, S. (2012) *Natural Childhood*. Wiltshire: National Trust/Park Lane Press.

Noren-Bjorn, E. (1982) *The Impossible Playground*. New York: Leisure Press.

Pretty, J., Angus, C., Bain, M., Barton, J., Gladwell, V., Hine, R., Pilgrim, S., Sandercock, S. and Sellens, M. (2009) *Nature, Childhood, Health and Life Pathways. Inter Disciplinary Centre for Environment and Society*. Occasional paper February 2009. Essex: University of Essex.

RSPB (2010) *Every Child Outdoors – Children Need Nature: Nature Needs Children*. Summary report, Sandy, Bedfordshire: RSPB. See www.rspb.org.uk

Siraj Blatchford, I., Sylva, K., Muttock, S., Golden, R. and Bell, D. (2002) *Researching Effective Pedagogy in the Early Years*. Research report 356. London: DfES (REPEY).

Tickell, C. (2011) *The Early Years: Foundations for Life, Health and learning – An Independent Report on the Early Years Foundation Stage to Her Majesty's Government*. (Also the Report on the Evidence, March 2011). See www.education.gov.uk

Tovey, H. (2007) *Playing Outdoors: Spaces and Places, Risk and Challenge*. London: Oxford University Press.

Vygotsky, L. S. (1978) *Mind and Society: The Development of Higher Psychological Processes*. Cambridge, MA: Harvard University Press.

Watts, A. C. (2011) *Every Nursery Needs A Garden*. London and New York: Routledge.

Appendix

Recipes for every season

- Spring vegetable chow mein
- Spring picnic sandwiches
- Spring birds' nests
- Summer berry shake
- Simple ice cream
- Summer fruit ice cream
- Summer fruit fool
- Monika's summer garden vegetable curry
- Summer pudding
- Summer new potato bake
- Autumn bonfire soup
- Autumn fruit crumble
- Pumpkin pie
- Autumn pumpkin soup
- Winter carrot and cream cheese cupcakes
- Winter sky, moon and stars (gingerbread version)
- Winter sky, moon and stars (shortbread version)
- Winter potato and leek pie

Spring vegetable chow mein

You will need

3 large spring onions
55g/2oz carrots
55g/2oz mushrooms
85g/3oz pak choi or Chinese leaves
55g/2oz mangetout
3 tbsp sesame oil
200g/7oz egg noodles
85g/3oz bean sprouts
4 tsbp soy sauce
Salt and pepper

Method

1. Children will be able to help with the preparation of the vegetables. Wash, dry and cut spring onions into thin slices. Cut or shred carrots. Cut mushrooms into thin slices. Cut Chinese leaves or pak choi into thin strips. Mangetout can be cut in half or left whole if preferred.

2. Heat oil in wok; add carrots, mangetout and spring onions. Stir fry for three minutes over a high heat.

3. Add noodles, bean sprouts, Chinese leaves or pak choi and mix together.

4. Season with salt and pepper, add soy sauce and drizzle over the sesame oil.

5. Mix together and stir fry for another three minutes.

This quantity will serve four adults but can be split into around twenty child-sized snack portions. Children can eat it either out of small bowls or plates, but will enjoy the challenge of using chopsticks.

Spring picnic sandwiches

Plan a spring picnic – if possible on a warm spring day, maybe sitting under a blossom tree, or if it's raining, erect a tarpaulin and children can listen to the raindrops as they eat.

You will need

Sliced bread
Low-fat spread
Sandwich filling
Cress (can be grown by the children at any time of year but is particularly easy in the spring; add to sandwiches for extra flavour)

Ham and cress filling

Use thin slices of ham and add cress.

Egg and cress filling

Hard boil four eggs, shell them and crush with a fork. Mix with a tablespoonful of milk and some mayonnaise until the mixture is easily spreadable.

Method

1. Children can butter the bread and will enjoy cutting off the crusts.
2. Add the filling.
3. Cut the sandwiches into fingers, triangles or squares (good for mathematical learning).

In the summer children can use any other salad crops they have grown such as lettuce, tomato and maybe even cucumber.

Spring birds' nests

You will need

50g/2oz butter
150g/5oz chocolate
3 tbsp syrup
5 Shredded Wheat
Bags of mini eggs – enough for two or three for each nest

Method

1. Melt butter, chocolate and syrup together in a bowl either over a pan of hot water or in the microwave for one to one and a half minutes on full power.

2. Crush the Shredded Wheat into another bowl or several smaller bowls if children have their own separate bowls.

3. Add the chocolate mixture and stir together. Spoon mixture into baking cases on a tray and make a dent in the middle for the eggs using the back of a teaspoon.

4. Allow to cool for an hour. Children can count and sort eggs into colour groups and put them in the nests. Makes 15 cakes.

Alternative microwave version

1 tbsp cocoa
75g/3oz golden syrup
100g/4oz butter, cut into small pieces
50g/2oz chocolate or chocolate buttons
4 Shredded Wheat (All-Bran can be used to give a more realistic nest)

1. Microwave the cocoa powder with the golden syrup, butter and chocolate for one and a half minutes.

2. Add crushed Shredded Wheat or All-Bran as above. Makes 12 cakes.

Summer berry shake

You will need

225g/8oz fresh or frozen mixed berries (to include strawberries, raspberries, blueberries and maybe some blackcurrants)
150g/5oz fruit-flavoured yoghurt, e.g. raspberry or strawberry
200ml/7fl.oz milk

Method

1. Children can help to wash and cut strawberries. Place the fruit and other ingredients in a blender and blend until smooth.

2. Serve in small beakers or paper cups.

Simple ice cream

You will need

Small (397g) tin of low-fat condensed milk
600ml double cream
1 tsp vanilla extract or half a vanilla pod (for vanilla ice cream)
Alternative flavouring such as chocolate, fresh strawberries or summer fruits could
be used

Method

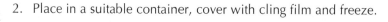

1. Put all the ingredients into a large bowl and beat with an electric whisk until
   it thickens.

2. Place in a suitable container, cover with cling film and freeze.

Summer fruit ice cream

This takes longer as it needs to be rebeaten, so may not be so good to use with children who are in a setting for a short space of time.

You will need

150g/5oz caster sugar
125ml/¼pt water
500g/1lb summer fruits: mix of strawberries, raspberries etc.
250ml/½pt double cream

Method

1. Make syrup by mixing the sugar and water in a pan over a low heat and boiling for three minutes.

2. Puree the fruit and mix with the syrup.

3. Whisk the cream in a separate bowl until it begins to thicken.

4. Add the cream to the cooled fruit mixture.

5. Pour into a suitable ice-cream container and freeze for about two to three hours. Then take out of freezer, empty into bowl and beat well again until smooth. Return mixture to the freezer.

Summer fruit fool

You will need

500g/1lb summer berries
200g/7oz fromage frais
150g/5oz plain low-fat yogurt
1 tsp honey

Method

1. Keep back a quarter of the fruit. Mash the remaining fruit with a fork or puree it with a hand blender. Mix with fromage frais, yogurt and honey.

2. Spoon into small individual cups and decorate with the remaining fruit.

3. Makes approx eight to ten small child portions, depending on size of container.

Monika's summer garden vegetable curry

Children at Tunstall Nursery spent two sessions preparing this healthy home-grown curry!

The first session was spent outdoors with children harvesting anything they have grown through the season. They usually pick spinach, broad beans, runner beans, tomatoes, chick peas, onions and carrots. They dig up potatoes and cut coriander. The potatoes are carefully sorted and washed. The vegetables are stored in the fridge overnight ready to cook the next day.

You will need

Vegetables: anything from your garden or supplement from a vegetable store if necessary. Try to include three carrots and two onions as the basic vegetables, and add anything else you have. Use a tin of tomatoes if you don't have many fresh ones.

Sunflower oil
2 vegetable stock cubes
1½ tsp garam masala
1½ tsp turmeric powder
2 litres/3½pt water (less if you don't have lots of vegetables or have a smaller pan)
Salt and pepper to taste

Method

1. Children cut up onions (lots of tears!), carrots and tomatoes.
2. Add these to a frying pan with some sunflower oil and cook gently until soft.
3. Transfer to a large saucepan and add the other vegetables, stock cubes, spices and water. Add salt and pepper if you wish.
4. Bring the mixture to the boil and cook slowly for about 25 minutes. Gently mash down the ingredients to make the curry.

At Tunstall they cook rice in a rice cooker and serve this with the curry in small disposable cups. Children love it!

©2013 Ann Watts, *Outdoor Learning through the Seasons*, London: Routledge.

Summer pudding

You will need

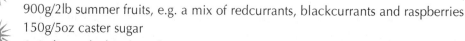
900g/2lb summer fruits, e.g. a mix of redcurrants, blackcurrants and raspberries
150g/5oz caster sugar
6–8 slices of white bread
850g/1.5pt pudding basin

Method

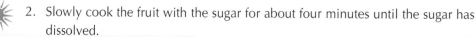

1. Children can help to prepare the fruit by removing stalks.
2. Slowly cook the fruit with the sugar for about four minutes until the sugar has dissolved.

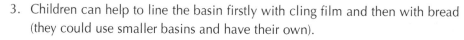

3. Children can help to line the basin firstly with cling film and then with bread (they could use smaller basins and have their own).
4. Press the bread together firmly to seal it. Add fruit and juice, then cover the basin with another piece of bread.

Place a plate or saucer that fits inside the rim of the bowl on top of the bowl and cool overnight in a fridge.

Turn the pudding upside down and serve the next day.

Summer new potato bake

If you are growing your own potatoes you will probably have lots of fairly small ones by the end of summer.

You will need

New potatoes
Fresh herbs
Olive oil
Fillings to serve (e.g. cheese, baked beans, tinned fish): optional

Method

1. Ask the children to help you to wash the potatoes thoroughly, then dry with tea towels or kitchen roll.

2. Thinly slice any larger potatoes or cut in half lengthwise. Prick the skins with a fork.

3. Collect some herbs from the garden, cut them as finely as possible and place in a roasting tin with a little olive oil.

4. Put tin in a preheated oven (200°C/400°F/Gas mark 6) to warm the oil and then add the potatoes.

5. Bake in the oven until they are tender (approx 25–30 minutes).

6. Split if they are large enough, then fill with grated cheese, baked beans or tuna, although they are delicious on their own.

Autumn bonfire soup

Children at Crosfield Nursery make this soup every year using ingredients of the same colours as the flames in their autumn bonfire. There is a laminated recipe book for children to follow, showing pictures of all the ingredients and what to do with them.

You will need

1 onion
2 medium-sized carrots
1 orange pepper
1 red pepper
1 yellow pepper
2 potatoes
4 large tomatoes
Small tin of tomatoes
1 vegetable stock cube and water

Method

1. Chop the onion, carrots, peppers and potatoes into small pieces. Place in pan with all the tomatoes.

2. Add stock and boil until vegetables are soft (around 20 minutes).

3. Blend in a mixer or blender, or leave as it is if preferred.

Autumn fruit crumble

You will need

3 large apples or 2 apples and a cupful of blackberries (or you can use 3 pears and maybe add a touch of cinnamon)
30ml/2 tbsp water
60ml/4 tbsp sugar for fruit
60g/2oz butter or margarine
125g/4oz plain flour
60g/2oz sugar for crumble mix

Method

1. Preheat the oven to 180°C/350°F/Gas mark 4.

2. Wash and chop the fruit. If using blackberries, remove all the stalks.

3. Place fruit and water in a large pie dish. Sprinkle with the sugar.

4. Make the topping by rubbing the butter into the flour until the mixture resembles coarse breadcrumbs. Add sugar and mix in well. Use demerara if possible, otherwise white is fine.

5. Bake in the oven for approximately 35 minutes until the top is golden brown.

Pumpkin pie

You will need

100g/4oz shortcrust pastry (it is easier to use ready-made pastry with children)
1kg/2lb fresh pumpkin
50g/2oz butter
100g/4oz caster sugar
½ level tsp salt
½ level tsp ground cinnamon
½ level tsp ground nutmeg
½ level tsp cloves (optional)
3 eggs, lightly beaten
150ml/¼pt single cream

Method

1. Preheat the oven to 400°F/250°C/Gas mark 6.

2. Roll out the pastry to a 23cm (9 inch) circle and use it to line a 20cm (8 inch) flan tin or pie dish.

3. Scoop out all the seeds and flesh from the pumpkin. (The seeds can be roasted in a hot oven for about 20 minutes to make a delicious healthy snack.)

4. Chop the pumpkin flesh into small pieces and put in pan with butter.

5. Cook until soft, then puree in blender.

6. Add sugar, salt and spices, then the beaten eggs and cream.

7. Pour the mixture into the pastry case and cook in the centre of the oven for about 40 minutes or until the filling has set.

Autumn pumpkin soup

You will need

A pumpkin around 4kg/9lb in weight
2 large onions
125g/4oz butter
1.7 litres/3pt chicken or vegetable stock
142ml/¼pt double cream or large carton of natural yogurt (optional)
Salt and pepper

Method

1. Cut the top off the pumpkin. Scoop out the seeds and fibres from the middle. (Pumpkin seeds can be roasted in the oven to make a delicious healthy snack.)

2. Hollow out the pumpkin to remove the flesh. Children enjoy this but may need some help! Chop the pumpkin flesh into small pieces.

3. Fry the onions in the butter until soft, remove from frying pan and place in a large saucepan with the pumpkin flesh and stock. Bring to the boil, boil for about ten minutes, and then when cool, add the cream or yogurt and put through a blender or mixer.

4. Add salt and pepper to taste.

Winter carrot and cream cheese cupcakes

You will need

125g/4oz soft butter
125g/4oz soft light brown sugar
Juice and finely grated rind of one orange
2 eggs, slightly beaten
175g/6oz grated carrots
125g/4oz self-raising flour
2 tsp mixed spice
1½ tsp baking powder

Method

1. Preheat the oven to 180°C /350°F/Gas mark 4.

2. Ask the children to put 12 (24 for double quantities) cup-cake cases in a bun tray or use double paper cases on a greased baking sheet.

3. Children can help to grate carrots and then weigh out 175g for the recipe.

4. Put the butter, sugar and orange rind in a bowl. Beat together until fluffy and light.

5. Add the eggs one at a time, beating in between. Add the orange juice and carrots.

6. In a separate bowl mix the flour, spice and baking powder and then fold in into the carrot mixture. Spoon the mixture into the cases.

7. Bake for approximately 20 minutes. Cool on a wire rack.

©2013 Ann Watts, Outdoor Learning through the Seasons, London: Routledge.

To make the cream cheese topping
You will need

125g/4oz butter or soft spread
350g/12oz cream cheese
1 tsp lemon juice or 1 tsp vanilla essence
125g/4oz icing sugar
marzipan and food colourings (optional; to decorate)

Method

1. Beat the butter until soft, add the cream cheese and lemon or vanilla flavouring, then slowly add the icing sugar, beating all the time.

2. The children may enjoy using marzipan to roll and shape into tiny carrots to decorate the cakes. These can be coloured with edible orange food colouring and if you are really ambitious, supply some green marzipan paste to make the carrot tops.

Winter sky, moon and stars (gingerbread version)

You will need

60g/2oz butter or margarine
125g/4oz soft dark brown sugar
60ml/4 tbsp golden syrup
225g/8oz plain flour
10ml/½ tsp ground ginger
2.5ml/½ tsp cinnamon
1 egg, beaten
Moon- and/or star-shaped cutters
Icing and sprinkles to decorate

Method

1. Preheat the oven to 190°C/375°F/Gas mark 5. Grease one or two baking trays.

2. Melt the sugar, butter or margarine and golden syrup in a pan.

3. Add the remaining ingredients and stir to make a soft dough. Add extra flour if it is sticky.

4. Allow it to cool and then let children roll it out on a floured surface and cut with star- and/or moon-shaped cutters.

5. Place on baking tray and bake for ten minutes or until firm to touch.

6. Cool on a wire rack and then decorate with white icing or sprinkle with white icing, edible glitter or rainbow dust.

Winter sky, moon and stars (shortbread version)

This recipe can be used to make any shape of shortbread biscuit. Shortbread fingers are a good gift for parents for Christmas or Mother's Day. Stars can also be used as winter decorations.

You will need

225g/8oz butter
125g/4oz caster sugar
350g/12oz plain flour
Moon- and/or star-shaped cutters
Icing sugar, icing, sprinkles etc. to decorate

Method

1. Preheat the oven to 190°C/375°F/Gas mark 5.

2. Cream the butter and sugar together in a large bowl, or divide into smaller, equal parts for children to use in individual bowls.

3. Add flour, slowly mixing in after each addition.

4. Knead into a ball and when it is firm, roll it out to no more than 1cm/½ inch thickness.

5. Use moon- and star-shaped cutters to make around 40 biscuits, depending on the size of the cutter.

6. Place the biscuits on a greased baking tray and put into oven for around 20 minutes or until golden brown. Cool on a wire rack. (N.B. Biscuits can be sprinkled with caster sugar if you wish to make a classic shortbread and left in the fridge to cool for 20 minutes before baking.)

7. Dust with sieved icing sugar when cool, or decorate with icing and silver decorations or edible glitter to make them twinkle.

Winter potato and leek pie

You will need

1kg/1lb potatoes, peeled and thinly sliced
1 small leek
120g/4oz broccoli or cauliflower florets (optional)
2 sliced tomatoes
60g/2oz grated cheese
2 eggs
300ml/½pt milk

Method

1. Preheat the oven to 200°C/400°F/Gas mark 6.

2. Precook the potatoes, boiling them in a pan of water for ten minutes. When they are cool let children help to slice them.

3. Cut leeks into thin slices.

4. Place sliced potatoes to cover the base of an ovenproof dish.

5. Cover with leeks, broccoli and tomatoes.

6. Arrange remaining potatoes on top and add grated cheese.

7. Beat the eggs with the milk and pour over the pie.

8. Cover with foil and bake for 45 minutes.

9. This dish can be used as a main meal or divided into small portions for use at snack time.